OTHER WORKS BY SUMMER BRENNER

**FICTION**

The Soft Room

Dancers and the Dance

One Minute Movies

I-5, A Novel of Crime, Transportation, and Sex

Nearly Nowhere

My Life in Clothes

Do You Ever Think of Me? (vol. 1)

The Missing Lover, collages by Lewis Warsh

**NOVELS FOR YOUTH**

Richmond Tales, Lost Secrets of the Iron Triangle

Ivy, Homeless in San Francisco

Oakland Tales, Lost Secrets of The Town

**POETRY**

Everyone Came Dressed as Water

From the Heart to the Center

# Dust

*A Memoir*

Summer Brenner

Spuyten Duyvil
New York City

© 2024 Summer Brenner
ISBN 978-1-959556-46-6
Cover painting: "David" by Rita Abelman Brenner (c. 1965)
Cover design: Joanna Bean Martin, Afterall Studio, Portland, OR

Library of Congress Cataloging-in-Publication Data

Names: Brenner, Summer, author.
Title: Dust / Summer Brenner.
Description: New York City : Spuyten Duyvil, 2024.
Identifiers: LCCN 2023039869 | ISBN 9781959556466 (paperback)
Subjects: LCSH: Brenner, Summer. | Authors, American--20th
  century--Biography. | American literature--Jewish authors.
Classification: LCC PS3552.R386 Z46 2024 | DDC 813/.54
  [B]--dc23/eng/20231010
LC record available at https://lccn.loc.gov/2023039869

For my brother
*David Randolph Brenner*
October 24, 1949 - October 15, 2002

*The old people in a new world, the new people made out of the old. That is the story that I mean to tell, for that is what really is and what I really know.*

—Gertrude Stein

# FOREWORD

My brother David and I were born to a Jewish family in Atlanta in the 1940s. Who knows why a thing roots in memory, but my early consciousness was formed by corners of wool blankets sucked until the fiber shredded; sheets hung over card tables to make hiding places; knees skinned raw in tomboy pursuits; a deep bond with my cousin Nancy; summer nights on sweat-drenched pillows; a recurring nightmare of being chased; the delight of nakedness; deep loneliness; and books, books, books. Like most siblings, David and I played together. But more often, I was alone.

Since his birth, David lived with mental and physical limitations. I served as his translator, interpreter, ally, and protector until I chose to leave. At eighteen I moved away for school and traveled, returning several times until I left to go west, first to New Mexico and then northern California.

In April 1973, I was called home from San Francisco. David refused to leave his apartment. He was having a breakdown. Eventually, he was diagnosed with schizophrenia, a malady that ended his autonomous selfhood. Afterwards he was cared for and confined in mental hospitals, halfway houses, and group homes in Georgia. Other than brief visits, phone calls, birthday cards, and gifts, I lived apart from David and our mother for thirty years. Then, through a series of events, both calamitous and miraculous, David came to live with me.

# PART 1

# THE BEGINNING

*Remember my little granite pail?*
*The handle of it was blue.*
*Think what's got away in my life!*
*Was enough to carry me thru.*

—Lorine Niedecker

Summer and David Brenner (circa 1950)

# 1

# THE GRAVE

When I first arrive, I wander through Plot #30. A man sits nearby. He's weeding a grave and crying. I feel I should leave him alone. I should abandon my search for David in case it's too close to the spot he has already claimed for his grief.

But David is not in plot #30. I find him in Plot #29, Space #7 (organized something like Chapter and Verse). He lies on a hill facing southwest, a hill dotted with majestic trees. Around us are the tombs of many. It's a populous village of notables. I deliberately chose to place my humble brother among them.

I sit on David's grave.

*May the mothers and fathers*
*who have lived and died*
*before us bless this spot.*

*May the children who are*
*yet to come revere it.*

David is in his plein-air closet. Narrow and contained, solid with earth below and infinity above. Across the blue firmament, wisps of fuzzy clouds hurry by. A perfect coverlet. The rectangle of grassy turf has nearly healed. It is nearly seamless. From the site, I can see a wedge of bridge and ship rigging.

Before he died, I asked David if he wanted to see the place. Then I quickly apologized, in case he found the suggestion morbid.

David said he was used to everything. I thought he meant that people had always said cruel and careless things to him. But maybe he meant he was untroubled by the prospect of death.

He declined to visit the cemetery and soon grew too sick to walk. However, I was able to show him photos in a brochure because Mountain View is a famous place. It's an historical landmark (1863) with mausoleums and obelisks, a bird sanctuary, and a beautiful, tranquil park, designed by the landscape architect Frederick Law Olmsted.

The bareness of the plain grass by David's grave is a comfort. By choice there is no container for flowers. The next time I bring flowers I'll simply lay them on the grass, so they can wither and blow away.

*May the plants*
*on this hillside provide*
*beauty for the living.*

*May the birds who pass*
*take note of its serenity.*

At the graveside funeral, there was only one bouquet. It was brought by young Zia, dressed in high-laced boots and a gray flannel smock. Throughout the service she cradled the white star-burst chrysanthemums. Then as we left the grave, she carefully—careful in the way children do solemn things for the first time—set them down by the pit. Formal flowers, they looked like fireworks that burst, then arc, then spray across the sky.

It is two weeks since David passed away. I sit and pluck the grass, while tears squeeze through their tiny ducts. A couple slip from the corners of my eyes onto my cheeks.

He is fortunate his suffering of nearly an entire lifetime has ended. He is fortunate to miss what might be coming. He's fortunate to miss the coming war. From now until we die, it looks as if we'll have to live in fear, made to believe that strangers want to hurt us, and constantly afraid to lose those we love.

I do not have definite beliefs. My beliefs are only indefinite. When I first saw him after he died, I thought he was alive because his face was restful and young. The terrible effort of breathing had ended.

Thank god, I thought. The terrible breathing is over, and now he is calm.

I didn't believe he was dead. Naively, I thought the rasp had stopped as a sign of wellness, recovery, health. For a few moments, he looked alive. He looked as he was meant to before life damned him.

After a short time, his eyes hollowed out into two black cavities. Suddenly, they were holes, not eyes at all, as if a vulture had snuck in and gobbled them. That is when his spirit flew out of that terrible, useless body.

But where did it go? That's what I mean by *indefinite*.

I look down into the grass, the dirt, the traces of insect life. I try to see him below me, his emaciated frame and queer face, his pale blue eyes, his boney tobacco-stained fingers in perpetual motion. I try to hear him singing, stumbling through the words, improvising and repeating *lalalalalala* like a tipsy Sinatra.

With concentration I peer through the stems of dry grass. Through the busy labyrinth of earth. And planks of hewn pine where there are already holes. The shroud, the hair, the epidermis, the bones, everything has holes. Soon they will grow lacy, each in their own way. The cotton shroud will separate into fibers and make a web. The little hair will vanish. The dry, hide-like skin will separate and then altogether disappear. The porous bones will whiten, polished by chewing and gnawing. The bones will remain, lying in their proper position, the pattern of a man. *Homo sapiens sapiens.*

I cry and pray.

*May the end of his life be a blessing.*
*May I someday find consolation.*

I think a shroud is fitting attire. He left the house in a shroud, and it made him look holy. I regard him as holy. And since I see him everywhere, I have begun to think of him as a god.

# 2

# DAVID COMES

It's a warm day in late October. The plaid drapes that hang by the front windows are pushed aside. These are the drapes my mother would have chosen with her decorator at Porter and Porter. Around the room the dark furniture is dusted and polished, the pillows plumped on the sofa and chairs, the ashtrays on the end tables wiped clean. It's called the "living room," but it's usually empty. An empty, lifeless room with no smells of humans, plants, food, or pets. It's only used for an occasional party when my parents serve drinks and hors d'oeuvres. After parties I go around and eat the crumbs. I lick the inside of the small liqueur glasses. The drops make my tongue burn.

It is hard for a child to wait, but I am vigilantly waiting. I stand by the window, hiding like a bat inside the drape. I can smell my breath. I can smell my starched dress and the sweat on my palms. I breathe on the window glass. The pane turns cloudy with my breath. I breathe harder. An entire square fogs. Then I wet my finger and make the letters I have only recently learned to write—

D - A

I pronounce the name in my head, trying to find the next sound. I hear the sound. My barley-size teeth bite hard on my lip to say it. "V," I say. It's my favorite letter to say aloud and write—

D - A - V

As soon as one letter is made on the windowpane, another evaporates. I exhale on the glass and start again—

D - A - V

"Where you?" a voice barks. Feet thump on the carpet.

I jump and duck my head deeper into the furl of drape. My eyes shut as I shrink to the size of a bug. I am hoping to disappear. But instead, I'm found.

"Getchaself outtathere!" the bark again.

Two white oxfords appear beneath the hem of the drape. I see brush strokes from white polish on the oxfords. They look dusted in chalk. A small hole has been cut from the left shoe's outside edge. Through the hole sticks a brown toe. Sitting on top of the toe like a brown derby is a hard, bumpy, swollen thing. A bunion, it's called. I try to avoid looking at it. But sometimes I can't help myself. Sometimes my eyes automatically look at the bunion.

My white leather shoes are also chalky from coats of polish. Stippled over the toe box is a design. The little holes make a design like a plume or a flower. When I asked about the holes, I was told, "They let your feet breathe." That's when I first learned that feet have to breathe.

"Out!" the voice with the bunion commands.

Since Mother went to the hospital, Mae has been in the house to take care of me. I couldn't visit Mother in the hospital. I had to wait at home. Mae is here all day. She'll stay on to help with the new baby. She's a practical nurse. That's why she wears a white uniform and white oxfords.

"Out!" she repeats.

I shed myself from the drape to see her jack-o'-lantern face above me. I understand the reason for her anger—my wrinkled dress, my disheveled hair, the tangled drape, my spit on the glass.

She has no praise for my writing. She wipes my letters off the window with her apron. She rakes her fingers through my hair. She smooths my dress. She motions for me to sit.

*I am a child*, I want to say in protest. But it is precisely my inferior status that puts me within her control.

"Sit or else the bogeyman gon' take you," she says.

She often tells me that if I don't obey, the bogeyman will take me. When she first told me, I believed her. It's because I believed everyone. I thought everyone told the truth. Maybe that's why children are called *innocent*. Maybe gullibility and innocence are the same.

The first time I heard about the bogeyman, I began to ask my mother if I'd been good. Every night before bed, I asked her.

"Yes," she said, "you're a good girl."

It was a nightly ritual. I never told her the reason I asked. I couldn't tell her. If I spoke the bogeyman's name, I was afraid he'd hurt me. Or her.

On a day after I'd been naughty, Mother refused to tell me. I cried. I begged. I pleaded. Nothing moved her to tell me that I'd been good. She sent me to bed where I cried myself to sleep. The next morning I was surprised. I didn't expect to find myself at home. I expected to find myself in the bogeyman's cave. After that I didn't believe in the power of the bogeyman.

However, other things scare me, especially the wall of windows in our den. The windows open to a woods at the back of the yard. At night the glass rectangles flicker like cages. At night I see a wild animal in each cage. Lions, tigers, monkeys, bears, they claw and climb the glass.

Suddenly, our car swings into the driveway. I jump from the chair. I clutch my elbows against my ribs and jump up and down with excitement.

"They're here!" I shout.

No one can restrain me now.

I yank on the brass knob and fly through the door.

Down the walkway, I run past the dogwood tree. Its leaves have started to fall. They curl like dry skins of old tangerines. It's October, and the leaves are on the grass.

I fly to the car. I stretch out my arms as I tumble down the flagstone steps. I am singing.

*A baby is coming*
*A baby boy is coming*
*A baby boy named David*
*He's coming to live with me!*

I sing because this moment is the most precious of my whole life.

Daddy has explained that our parents make David and me nearly the same. He is *my* brother, son of Rita and Eddie. I am *his* sister, daughter of Rita and Eddie. Rita and Eddie made us. We're baby brother and big sister forever connected. He belongs to no other girl. He's mine. Now I will have a living doll to dress and feed. To carry and drag around. I won't be an only child. I won't be the only one.

Daddy turns off the car. Through the window Mother holds up a small bundle.

"See," she smiles.

I can't see much.

When Daddy opens the door for Mother, I fall forward. I try to kiss and hug them.

"Let me carry him! Let me! LET ME!" I shout.

There's a warning look. I'm too close. I'm crowding them.

Daddy helps Mother. She is tired. She has been to the hospital. I understand that it's a huge thing to have a baby. That it's the hugest thing of all.

*My brother*
*in heaven*
*sent to us*
*in Mother's tummy.*

While Mother was in the hospital, I thought something bad might happen to her. I cried in my sleep that she died. I prayed she wouldn't die. I'm relieved to see that she's alive. The small bundle is alive. They're both safe at home.

We head back to the house. Mother carries the baby. Daddy carries me. They don't let me touch him. They think I'm dirty. They think I'll drop him.

"I'm not dirty," I say to Daddy.

And then in the air with my finger, I draw the cryptic shapes—

D - A - V - I - D

# 3

# THE TOY STORE

In summer the daylight is nearly white. Its color is dulled by the flat, hot, heavy air. The sky and sun are buried in a white vapor that hangs like a starched sheet. The thick air presses down on everything. The nearby objects—my red wagon, my parents' blue car, the houses—pulse with the heat around them. From the road, the asphalt sends up zigzag waves of heat.

David and I don't care. We squat in the yard and pick at our scabs. We whisper under the shade of the dogwood tree.

Around the curves of Buckhead's hills, Grandpa is coming. We're in the yard waiting for him. He grins when he drives up in his big Cadillac, weaving like a madman from left to right and right to left, nearly crashing into the curb.

Grandpa is old and white-haired. He's so jolly it scares me.

"He's dangerous when he drives," Mother laughs.

Grandpa stops in front of our house. He stares at us, wondering if we're the right children. He toots his horn, tapping lightly. Then he pushes his hand down so the horn blasts through the thick air. I wonder if it's safe to get into Grandpa's car, but Mother shoos us along.

Our cousins Nancy and Sally are in the backseat. We climb in beside them. We sit on the dove-gray upholstery as soft as fur. In the front seat, their older brother Larry sits next to Grandpa. He's pretending to drive, pretending to be grown up. We don't like Larry because he is big and never kind. Whenever he gets the chance, he throws firecrackers at us from the roof of my aunt's house.

From Habersham Road, it's not far to the toy store on Roswell. Grandpa asks each of us to pick out a toy. He marches up and down the aisles like a general, playing with marionettes, dump trucks, sailboats, kites, and miniature cars. He marvels at everything.

I want David to choose the jack-in-the-box, but every time it pops up, he starts to cry.

Larry picks out a model plane. My cousins like stuffed animals and dolls. I choose a stamp-collecting book. The book comes with a package of stamps in crayon colors—coral, turquoise, lavender, lime. The stamps have strange letters, strange money signs, strange patterns. I like the cancelled stamps best. I like the black concentric lines. They make me imagine the stranger who wrote the letter. She or he wrote it in a foreign language. They licked a foreign stamp. They dropped it off to mail in a foreign land. Stamps are proof of other places. Places where everything is different.

Josh is our collie. Josh pushes David down if he tries to run into the street.

"Collies are smarter than most men," Daddy says. "The only bad thing about collies is they think that cars are sheep. It's the reason they chase cars."

I can't tell if that's smart or not.

"We were going to name your brother either David or Joshua," Daddy says.

Since they chose David for my brother, we call our dog Josh. It's odd to consider that they're equal—my brother and my dog. Or maybe Daddy is joking. Maybe they always meant to call my brother David. These kinds of questions fly through my mind, but I don't know how to say them. Or whom to say them to.

Sadly, Daddy is right about collies. Josh is hit by a car and killed.

# 4

# EARLY YEARS

When we drive to Grandpa's mill, it takes a long time. It's not far, but it's another world. Although it's near *downtown*, there are no stores. There are no restaurants, hotels, banks, or movie theaters. There is nothing but shacks and brick warehouses with corrugated steel roofs.

Close to Grandpa's mill are blocks of shacks. Some have no glass in the windows. Some have windows stuffed with rags and tar paper. Some have tar paper roofs. The yards are Georgia red clay, called *red* from iron oxide. When it rains, the water doesn't sink into the clay. Instead, it floods the unpaved streets and yards. Dry, the clay is copper color. Wet, it looks like blood. Some yards are bare, others filled with tires and old cars. Or tin cans with flowers set out around the door. For reasons I can't explain, the flowers make everything look worse.

When we drive to Grandpa's mill, I get down on the floor of the backseat. I hide on the floor. I hide because of our car, our house, our clothes. I'm a small child, but I see. Something is wrong. I see some people have a lot and others almost nothing. No one explains why. No one thinks a child is aware. Or needs to know. Or would care. I don't know how to say these things. Or whom to say them to. I don't know how to ask. I certainly can't ask my mother. She thinks I'm off my rocker to get on the floor of the car. She yells at me to get back into the seat. She yells that my dress will get dirty.

Thirty years later a friend tells me that when she was twelve, her bus to Manhattan detoured through Newark. She lived in a wealthy neighborhood in New Jersey, and on other trips the bus had never detoured. When Susan returned home, she asked her parents, "Who makes them live like that?" At five or six, this was the question I wanted to ask if I'd known how to find the words.

Grandpa's mill makes flour and chicken feed. The flour is packed in decorative cloth sacks. The sacks are cross-stitched at the top and printed with pictures. They can be saved and reused—for curtains or a tablecloth, for a shirt or a child's shift. Inside the mill is a test kitchen where Black women bake all day. They test recipes for pies, cakes, cookies, biscuits. Recipes are also printed on the flour sacks.

The mill is on Mangum Street, a narrow street where trucks rumble up and down. In front of the mill are loading docks stacked with sacks of flour and feed. Trucks and men sit around waiting to load and unload. PURITAN MILLS is chiseled over the entrance to the building. It's a modest entry and a musty building. I'm surprised that a fortune could be made in such a place.

Outside, the workers are Black. Inside, they're White.

There's a ring of desks with ladies, most of them old with tinted blue hair. On their desks are adding machines and candy bowls. They sit and punch numbers and keys. CA-CHINK! CA-CHINK! Loops of paper roll forward, loop after loop, tumbling around the floor like confetti.

Grandpa is a rich man. As a result, his daughters are rich, too. Mother is proud of her father's fortune. He left the Russian Empire with nothing. He arrived in Georgia with nothing. Now he has a custom-built Cadillac and a chauffeur. He winters in Miami Beach. He came with nothing, and now he has whatever he wants. His fortune even increased during the Great Depression. When so many people lost everything, Grandpa got richer. Daddy told me it was because people couldn't afford to buy bread. They could only afford to buy flour and make their own bread.

Grandpa's office is a world within a world. An inner sanctum away from the loading docks and smelly street. His large swivel chair is leather. His office walls are dark wood paneling covered with plaques and certificates. On top of the desk is a green baize pad and a marble stand to hold his gold pens.

Grandpa is always happy to see us. His blue eyes brighten when he sees us. He tosses his head of white hair like a happy old horse. He twists our cheeks, pinches our nose, and flaps his fingers across our lips. It's painful and unpleasant, but I accept it as a sign of Grandpa's love.

When the wind blows the wrong way, there's an awful smell at the mill. I feel sick when I smell it. Someone says the smell comes from a sausage factory. Someone else says it's a slaughterhouse. Or maybe they're the same thing. Whatever it is, it makes me gag.

On Sunday morning TV, and in between church services, three men in string ties huddle around a microphone. Two with guitars and one with a fiddle. It's a commercial break, and they sing a jingle about Puritan Mills. We don't watch the church service, only the commercial with the jingle.

*Migh-ty Pure / Self-rising flour!*
*Migh-ty Pure / Migh-ty Pure!*

The men look poor. White poor, not Black poor. I think White poor means people who hate Blacks. I've been taught that. I don't understand why Grandpa lets them sing his jingle.

Atlanta's *real* downtown has lots of stores, restaurants, hotels, banks, and movie theaters. The largest department store is Rich's, owned by a Jewish family. At the fanciest shops, like Frohsin's and J.P. Allen and the couture department at Rich's, the salesladies know my mother's name. When she waltzes in, they say, "Hello, Rita!" Or "Hello, Mrs. Brenner!" They know her taste. They know her size. They rush to bring out their most stylish dresses and coats, sweaters and slacks.

They often work on commission. They're eager to make a big sale.

Leb's is in downtown, too. Leb's is a large Jewish deli that serves corned beef and pastrami sandwiches on pumpernickel and rye. It serves bagels with cream cheese and lox. It has refrigerated glass cases with cold cuts, coleslaw, potato salad, large dill pickles, and cheesecake. It serves chicken soup with matzah balls or kreplach. It serves borscht. Customers sit on stools at a long counter, or at tables and booths. Leb's is a favorite restaurant for businessmen and women working in downtown. I like knowing that gentiles come to Leb's to eat Jewish food. It makes me feel closer to them.

"Jews from New York own Leb's." That's what Jews in Atlanta say. They want to make sure everyone knows there's a distinction. Jews in Atlanta aren't the same as Jews from New York. The implication is that Atlanta Jews are polite. They're mild-mannered and agreeable. They understand the conventions associated with race. All to imply that Jews from New York do not.

Whenever the KKK marches through downtown, they pass Leb's. They deliberately choose a route that passes Leb's. They wear long white robes and carry their hoods in their hands. They can't hide behind their hoods. There's a law now that makes them show their faces. The women also wear white robes and carry babies in tiny white outfits and pointed hoods like Halloween ghosts. I know about the KKK. I know they burn crosses and do things that I can't let myself imagine. I know they hate Jews. They hate Blacks, Catholics, and Jews. Because Daddy stands up for the rights of Blacks, I worry they'll come to our house. I worry they'll burn a cross in our yard.

At Leb's our family likes to sit in a booth by a window. If the Klan is marching, I see them through the window. They're grinning when they pass us. Or maybe *grin* is incorrect. Maybe *grimace* is the correct word. I see how proud and happy they are to march. I've been taught you're only supposed to be proud of good things. I wonder if they think they're good. I wonder if it makes them happy to hate.

5

# WORK AND PLAY

The streets in Ansley Park slope and curve under beautiful old trees, circling between Peachtree Street and Piedmont Park like a maze. Many of the old houses are large and handsome. They're situated by parks and a creek. But Ansley Park is slightly shabby. Despite the Governor's Mansion, it's no longer fashionable to live near downtown.

Mother's milliner lives in a big house in Ansley Park. It's light yellow brick with rooms full of love seats, chairs, and dainty tables with mirrors. Hats perch everywhere on racks and mannequin heads. Women sit and try on hats or thumb through magazines to find hats for the milliner to make. Mother tries on hats. She orders hats. Sometimes I play with the hats, admiring myself in the mirror.

Mother has a dressmaker, too. He lives in a modest house in Ansley Park, much smaller than the milliner's. He and Mother look at magazines. They critique the clothes in *Vogue* and *Harper's Bazaar*. He makes her a black organza sailor dress trimmed in gold braid. He makes her a cut-velvet suit. She has beautiful dresses: a black lace gown lined with chartreuse silk, a gray quilted satin, a parrot green chiffon. Mother dresses like a movie star.

"I'm so fond of him," she says about her dressmaker.

*Fond* is a different category of affection. *Fond* sounds a little strange. Only later do I realize he was gay. Married but gay. Throughout her life, Mother has a fondness for homosexuals. *Homos*, she calls them. They share a love for clothing, art, and decor. In turn, they're very fond of her.

I too have beautiful dresses. My favorite is apricot satin with flocked velvet brown leaves and a grosgrain belt. Sadly, a dress can't hide me. It can't hide my stick arms or stick legs, my undersized head or horsy teeth. I like books more than dresses. Inside books I can disappear.

On the other side of Ansley Park is Piedmont Park. Nearly two hundred acres of woods with a swimming pool, ball fields, a lake, playgrounds, tennis courts, and picnic areas. We don't swim in public pools because of polio. For swimming we go to a private club. However, we often visit the lake. We sit on swinging wooden benches. The benches have chains attached to the limbs of trees and long enough to swing out over the water. On hot days, it's always cool and shady. Blue shadows slide over the ground and water. It's a dark, mysterious place.

Mother reads. David and I gaze at the water and the lily pads in bloom. We watch the geese, ducks, and swans. Sometimes we play on the steep, slippery bank of the lake. We bring a loaf of stale Merita bread. After we break the bread into little pieces, we throw them in the water. Once they're in the water, the lake explodes. Birds rush towards the bread from every direction. They no longer care about swimming or gliding on the water. They crowd against each other. They snap and shove to get at the bread. It's supposed to be fun to feed the birds, but instead, it's sad. I don't know what to call it—hunger or greed, natural or manmade.

*

My first beach excursion is to Florida. Daddy and I go on an airplane to Miami. It's a rocky ride in a prop plane. So rocky that I vomit into the little airsickness bag. We visit my mother's parents, Anna and Morris. They're staying at a hotel on Miami Beach. We stay in the same hotel.

Although I can't read very well, I'm aware of the top story in the Miami newspaper. Two young sisters have drowned in a pool. Their father was training them to swim the English Channel. Their father wanted them to be the youngest swimmers to cross the Channel. Even when they begged him to stop, he made them practice. That's how they died. This is the first time I realize that children can die.

And there is something else, something vague and troubling. A question I can't articulate but nonetheless, it lingers in my mind for a long time. If you want to do something exceptional, something like break the record as the youngest person to swim the English Channel, do you have to push yourself to the brink of death?

*

On the first day of first grade, my teacher puts me in the corner. "You're too excited," she says. "You talk too much." Afterwards I try not to open my mouth. All year I barely say a word.

In second grade, the teacher asks, "Who are your parents voting for? The General or the Egghead?" Everybody but me raises their hand for General Eisenhower. Daddy loves Adlai Stevenson, the Egghead.

Third grade is my best year with my best friend Nan. But in summer Nan's family moves to a different house near a different school. I have to walk to Brownies alone. I don't like Brownies. I don't care about badges. When it's Mother's turn to bring snacks, she brings fruit and juice, not cookies and sodas. No one wants fruit and juice. Mother says they're healthy, but *healthy* doesn't count. At Brownies we practice what to do if someone catches on fire. I practice by throwing a bucket of water on another Brownie. I'm reprimanded. I'm told I was only supposed to pretend to throw the water. They think it was an accident. I'm not a very good Brownie.

Every night Daddy reads to me. In a big armchair, I sit on his lap while he reads. His lap is the safest place I know. Our favorite books are *Winnie the Pooh* and

*Mary Poppins*. Both are extremely amusing. Every week Mother takes me to the Buckhead library. She searches for grownup books to read, and I inspect the children's shelves. When she reads *Auntie Mame*, I read it, too. It's a naughty book that I'm not supposed to read.

Down a long, steep hill, I pedal as fast as I can. The wind blows my hair. The wind stings my skin. It's the most wonderful feeling. My first feeling of freedom. At the corner of Habersham and Valley roads, there's a creek. I stop to wave my hands in the ripples of water. Tadpoles swim between my fingers. They swim in unison like flocks of birds fly.

Ann is the new girl next door. We're almost the same age.

"Our neighbors are color blind," Ann tells me. "They painted their house baby blue and nigger pink."

I repeat what Ann says to Daddy. Daddy can't help himself. Daddy smacks me. I go flying across the room. Daddy says I must *never* use that word again.

When my cousin Nancy visits, we play in the yard. We let David follow us around. We all play together under the pines. We make houses with pine straw. We bring things from the kitchen and pretend this is where we live.

Scotty is our neighbor across the street. He's a year or two older. He asks Nancy and me to go into the woods behind my house. We don't let David come with us. We leave David behind. I like Scotty because he and his brother taught me to ride a bike. Not a bike for little kids but a big bike like they ride.

In the woods, Scotty asks us to pull down our panties. He pulls down his pants and underwear, too. I wish I hadn't pulled down my panties. But Nancy doesn't seem to mind. She's a few months older than me and more daring. When our maid finds us in the woods, she drags us home. She threatens to give us a switching. I think David tattled on us. I think he was afraid and told her where to find us.

Ann is not a nice girl. She throws her cat in Nancy's face. Ann knows we don't like cats. She knows we're dog people. Everyone knows dog and cat people are different. After she throws her cat at Nancy, I bite Ann's thigh. Her thigh feels like a hard apple. I sink my big teeth into her skin. It's a vicious bite. I'm not a very nice girl either.

Ann's mother calls me over to their house. I know I hurt Ann. I've seen the bruise on her thigh. But Ann's mother surprises me. She explains in a kind way that I've done a bad thing. I already know it's bad, but Ann's mother forgives me. From Ann's mother, I realize kindness is more powerful than punishment.

\*

We don't have birthday parties. It's too much trouble for Mother. "You don't have any friends to invite," Mother says. Instead, she buys a cake.

After dinner I'm supposed to make a birthday wish and blow out the candles. I always hesitate because making a wish is difficult. To make a wish worthy of a whole year is a big responsibility. I can think of only one worthy wish.

*No bombs*, I wish. *No bombs, no bombs, no bombs.*

Year after year, this is my birthday wish. It's forbidden to tell a wish. If you tell, it won't come true. There are other reasons I don't tell. My parents might think something is wrong with me. There's already something wrong with David. I'm supposed to be their normal child. I'm supposed to act normal. In many ways, I am normal. But my obsession with bombs isn't normal.

When I climb the dogwood tree in the front yard, I sing. I sing at the passing cars. I want to grow up and be a singer. Singing in the tree is the way I train for singing as an adult. I know the words to many sophisticated songs. Some words I don't understand. Cole Porter has many clever and suggestive lyrics that I don't understand. But if I miss the meaning of the words, I understand the feeling. I can sing for an hour without repeating a song.

*Some they may go for cocaine*
*I'm sure that if I took even one sniff*
*It would bore me terrifically too*
*Yet I get a kick out of you* . . . .

One afternoon David is playing in the basement

with Nancy and me. He tumbles off a ledge and cuts his head on the concrete floor. David's forehead is bleeding. Mother rushes him to the hospital for stitches. Despite the blood, it's not a bad cut. It's only a few stitches.

Later Mother tells me, "It's *your* fault if something is wrong with David."

I don't believe Mother. Before he fell, there was something wrong with David. Whatever is wrong with David, it's not my fault.

# 6

# OLD HOUSE, NEW HOUSE

I'm ten and David five when we move to a new house. We move from our *starter* house on Habersham Road to a much bigger house on Northside Drive. The new house is very old and very big. Before we move, it has to be readied—ochre paint rubbed into the dark oak-paneled walls, casement windows repaired, floors refinished, wallpaper pasted, rooms painted, and appliances installed. Furniture has to be bought. Mother consults with her decorator at Porter and Porter on dozens of items. It promises to be a showplace.

The new house sits on a rocky point, the highest point in Fulton County. In the distance, lights from the city twinkle like jewels. But beyond the French doors and windows, there's an almost impenetrable darkness. Few neighbors and few cars make it a lonely house. The largest rooms are rarely used. Mother might tinkle out a Gershwin tune on the baby grand, or I might practice piano and dance to LPs and 78s on the Victrola. Or my parents might play bridge with other couples. Otherwise, the formal living and dining rooms are never used.

We eat all our meals in the breakfast room. It's painted a cheerful yellow with windows that overlook a stone terrace and an overgrown ravine. Burlap panels of half-naked women hang on the yellow walls. Mother got the panels from a department store display. I worry what other kids will think of these bare-breasted women, but it's not a *real* concern. Hardly anyone comes to visit.

Family convening takes place in the library. An hexagonal room with two sides of built-in shelves for books. The warm hues of matching material on the couch, chairs, and drapes, the TV and fireplace make it the only cozy room in the house. In the evening, we watch TV. Our boxer Jigger joins us. If we watch "Lassie" or "Rin Tin Tin," Jigger lays his head on his front paws and tracks the dogs on TV. When the TV dogs run, Jigger's back legs twitch.

We didn't name our boxer "Jigger Sazerac Brandy." He came to us with that name. It's a name that I'm reluctant to say in front of others. I'm alarmed whenever I have to shout it. If Jigger runs after the school bus, I lean out the bus window and shout, "Go home, Jigger! Jigger, go home!" The other kids don't know what a jigger is. They think "Jigger" is a substitute for a bad word they commonly say. A word I'm forbidden to say. A word I would never say. Of all the dogs we have, Jigger is my favorite, but I wish he had a different name.

Mother thinks Daddy pays too much attention to me—and not enough to David. I am Daddy's little protégée. He and I play chess. He and I study the Encyclopedia Britannica. Sometimes we play a game where we slap each other's hands. I hover my hands on top of Daddy's while he tries to slap them. If he misses, then I get to slap his hands. He almost never misses. He slaps my hands before I can move them. He slaps until they're red and raw. He sometimes pretends to burn me. He puts his cigarette close to my skin and flicks his finger. I always jump. I always think I've been burned. I think of Daddy with the greatest affection, but I wonder about these games. The slapping and the burning. A little torturer lives inside Daddy. I guess a torturer lives inside me, too. I sit on my brother's chest and tickle him until he cries.

The main floor is a long, flat rectangle. Below it is the first floor that fits into a small hollow. On the first floor is a massive oak door with iron studs and a large iron knocker. The door opens onto a stone entryway and stone turret. Part fantasy, part utility, it makes the house look like a castle. On the first floor is also the children's wing—two bedrooms, a playroom, a dressing room, and a bathroom for David and me. The walls of my room are covered in blue *Toile de Jouy* with matching curtains and bedspread and an eyelet dust ruffle for my canopy bed. These too are formal, tidy rooms. There are no toys littered about. No games, no puzzles, no mess.

A short set of stairs leads up to the main floor with the library, the powder room, the living and dining rooms, the kitchen and butler's pantry, the maid's room and bathroom, and the back door where we typically go in and out of the house. A staircase inside the turret continues to the upper floors. The master suite is on the third floor. On the fourth floor is another bedroom and bath used by Daddy as an office or a refuge. He wants to be a writer. He goes up there to write and drink.

The yard is a mix of clay and rock. The lawn is a patch of crabgrass and a few shrubs, a pair of Japanese magnolias, a mimosa tree, and purple phlox which thrives on the rocks. Behind the house is a one-room cottage, built as an artist's studio with half-size rock walls, rough-hewn posts and rafters, plank floors, and a stone fireplace. Beside the cottage is a well. We depend on a well for our water. David and I explore the hill behind the house. We find remnants of terraced beds with irises and roses. We too have a "secret garden."

There is much to marvel at, but I never feel *at home*. I never feel comfortable. I often dream of other houses where I could live. I grow up equating big houses with loneliness and despair. I later learn that the site was a redoubt during the Civil War. As the highest point for miles, it was a strategic lookout. Its rocks were later used to build our house, each rock tainted with war.

In Buckhead our maid came by bus across town. She came in the morning and left in the afternoon. Buses to Buckhead were filled with Black women, coming and going. Some in uniform, some not. The new house is too far outside the city limits for bus service. Our maid now lives with us in a bedroom on the far side of the kitchen. She lives with us and makes the beds. She washes, irons, and puts away the clothes. She vacuums and sweeps.

She cooks the meals and polishes the silver. She does everything, and we do nothing. She's paid, yes. She has free room and board and her own bathroom, yes. But we're not a very nice family. I wonder how she tolerates Mother's temper, David's fits, Daddy's drinking, and me.

None of the hired help stays long. Maybe the pay is too low. Or the house too remote. Beautiful Tina stays a year. Five nights a week, she occupies her meager room like a queen. Tina is so beautiful that it's painful to watch her work. She should be a movie star, not a maid.

At night I travel through the dark, haunted rooms, past the white marble fireplace that shimmers. Past the gilded mirror that reflects the marble. Past the dark kitchen to Tina's room.

I knock timidly. "Tina, can I come in?"

Tina is resting. She's stretched out on the narrow bed, her sinuous form curled in repose. Her straightened hair picturesquely arranged on the pillow.

I take a reverential seat by Tina's feet. She speaks to me about this and that—her children in South Carolina, her boyfriend who's a city cop, her parents in another part of the state. I listen and stare at the fur covering her long, shapely legs. She tells me she doesn't shave because of her boyfriend.

"He loves feelin' my legs," she tells me.

This is my initiation to sexual desire. An inkling of what adults like to do to each other. Sometimes Tina lifts her hair from her neck and lets me touch the pair of crescent keloid scars. At the back of her neck, her husband pushed a knife right to left. Her sister took it out.

"Like a butter knife," she tells me.

I think my parents' fights are brutal, but this is attempted murder.

After Tina leaves, Cora comes. She's as skinny as a stick, and her face and arms are scarred with tiny pink spots. The pigment was burned off in an explosion. Cora doesn't cook well, not like Marian at my aunt's house. She only cooks country food.

"Hick food," Mother says. "We don't eat that." Mother teaches Cora how to cook our kind of food.

The worst thing about Cora isn't cooking. It's her snuff. All day she keeps a lump of snuff tucked in her lip or cheek. The snuff makes Cora drool. She constantly has to wipe brown drool from the corners of her lips. Mother doesn't mind Cora's snuff. She and Cora have a bond. Cora is Mother's ally.

My cousin Nancy's family is moving, too. Their new house is under construction. A split-level modern house with travertine floors, sliding glass doors, an indoor fish pond with orange carp and plants called birds-of-paradise. When their family moves, Marian will move with them. Marian will have her own room next to the kitchen. Marian has been with my aunt's family for years. She stays throughout my cousins' childhood. She raises Larry, Nancy, and Sally. She partly raises me, too.

Like our house on Habersham Road, my aunt's *starter* house is for sale. It's across from Peachtree Creek and the Bobby Jones Golf Course. Nancy and I can't play in the creek. We've been warned there's quicksand in the creek. If you step in quicksand, you don't go down at once. You go down slowly. The more you struggle to get out, the deeper you sink. When I was very young, I saw a horror movie with quicksand. A babysitter let me watch it. I never forgot the bubbles at the end of the film where the two villains sank.

Both our houses are open on Sunday. My mother's and my aunt's. It's called Open House. They're open so interested buyers can look around. One Sunday my aunt's family returns to find their house surrounded by police. Their yard is cordoned off. Their realtor has been shot. She has been found dead in the basement.

Later the police look for the gun in the creek. They dredge the creek. The gun and killer are never found.

# 7

# CURSES AND GHOSTS

My view of reality is reversed—sleeping is my real life and daytime is a dream. Before I'm able to sleep, I have to check everything. I check beneath the dust ruffle under the canopy bed. I get out of bed and check the built-in closets in the dressing room. I straighten the hangers. I refold the sweaters. I rearrange the shoes in the shoe cubby. I open and close the drawers of the dressing table. I check the bathroom that divides my room from David's. Over and over, I straighten and check. I check ten or more times. I put everything in order to prepare for my *real* life. Only later do I learn that this is a mental disorder. An aberrant form of behavior that has a name. A syndrome with an acronym.

The old school was in Sandy Springs. It bused in farm kids from Roswell. It had a 4-H Club. A new school built near our house draws from new suburban neighborhoods. At the old school, there were no Jews. At the new school, when I'm absent on Rosh Hashanah, Ellen Kahn asks me if I'm Jewish. She tells me she has been absent, too.

Ellen lives in a sprawling one-story house. Like our house, it's large and formal. But warmer and calmer. Ellen lives with her parents and brother in one wing. Her

Nana lives in the other. When I spend the night, we visit Nana in her sitting room. On Saturday mornings, Nana is on a small sofa, wrapped in a mohair shawl. Next to the sofa is a radio tuned to the weekly broadcast of the Metropolitan Opera in New York. Her favorite composer is Wagner. Ellen's mother's favorite composer is Wagner. They both love opera. Before I met Ellen's family, I never knew Jews liked anything German.

At Ellen's house are a cook, a maid, and a chauffeur. The chauffeur's name is Noble. He smells like whiskey. When he drives Ellen and me to dancing class, we can smell it. He waits outside while we learn to fox trot and cha-cha-cha. Ellen and I want Terry to ask us to dance. Terry doesn't look like a nice Jewish boy. He looks like a greaser, with pimples and a line of fuzz above his lips. He has sex appeal. But Terry wants to dance with Susan and Meredith. Both are blond with luscious breasts. In my brown velvet party dress, I have no sex appeal. I'd like another kind of dress, something updated for dancing class. Mother says the velvet dress was expensive. She calls it *getting your money's worth.*

"Y'all know what *nookie* is?" Noble asks us.

We have no idea.

"If y'all don't know now, y'all gonna know someday," Noble says.

*Nookie? Nooky?* Silently, we repeat the two syllables in our head so we can look it up in the dictionary.

Daddy takes Ellen and me to Gainesville for the

Miss Georgia Chick contest. Gainesville is the "Chicken Capital of the World." Daddy is one of the contest's judges. Since Puritan Mills sells chicken feed, Daddy is asked to be a judge. The other judges predict I'll someday be a contestant for Miss Georgia Chick. It seems highly unlikely, but they give me the same silver cuff bracelet that real contestants get. The winner gets money, a Miss Georgia Chick crown, a bouquet of flowers, and a box of fluffy golden baby roosters. Otherwise, I'm told the roosters would be ground up for fertilizer. I picture a garbage disposal for baby roosters—like the giant toaster I once pictured as the electric chair that killed Ethel and Julius Rosenberg.

The new house and new school are close to Lockheed Marietta. Military jets often fly over, breaking the sound barrier. BOOM! If there's a war with the USSR, Lockheed is a major strike point. Lockheed means I have to wear a dog tag with my name, address, and religion pressed into the metal.

I ask the teacher why we have to wear it.

"To help identify our bodies," she says.

She looks pained when she says these words. It pains her to suggest our bodies will be unrecognizable. Another student asks if she hates Russians. This is a painful subject, too. She explains that Russian people are different from the Russian government. She says Russian people are similar to Americans.

I'm afraid my teacher is a Communist. When I tell

Daddy, he reassures me. But I have doubts about Daddy. He doesn't like the government. He doesn't like the President. He hates General MacArthur and Henry Luce. He doesn't believe in God. He's against Zionism. He's upset about the treatment of Blacks. He's called a "nigra lover" and a "pinko." I'm afraid he's a Communist, too.

My brother goes to a special school. *Special*, these students are called. In this case, *special* doesn't sound good. After school he goes to speech therapy and a psychiatrist. Every day Mother helps him with his homework. It's torture for David. She yells when he misses a word. She makes him repeat his multiplication tables until he cries. She believes she's helping him. She believes this is the only way David will learn.

There's something wrong with David, but no one talks about it. If you hint that something might be wrong, Mother gets hysterical. Whenever I try to puzzle out David's affliction, bad luck is my only explanation.

"Everyone in our family has bad luck," Mother likes to say.

Almost all of Mother's time is spent "helping" David. She leaves me alone. Bad luck for David, good luck for me. I try to stay out of her way in my room. I read as much as possible. Sometimes I take a book to the table. I try to read at meals, but I'm usually foiled. I love the expression *bookworm*. I'm a bonafide bookworm.

When I'm older, I have a school assignment to read *Lord Jim*. On the night I finish, Daddy comes into my room. He finds me sobbing.

"I've just finished *Lord Jim*," I explain.

"Was it so sad?" he asks.

Conrad's books are sad. Or maybe tragic is more apt. But that's not why I'm sad.

"It's because I finished," I tell Daddy. *Lord Jim* is a book I never wanted to end.

Daddy rarely comes home for dinner. I wonder if he's really working. I worry that he's out drinking. When he's home, Mother wants us to perform for him. She wants to show off how smart David is. That's why she yells at David. She wants David to impress Daddy. Mother has read that whistling is a sign of intelligence. She asks Daddy to listen to us whistle. I already know the outcome. David can't whistle at all, and I'm a poor whistler. When I fail, Mother is pleased. It proves to Daddy that I'm not so smart.

On Sunday morning, Daddy drives to the Jewish deli. Sometimes David and I ride with him. Not Leb's in downtown but another deli on West Paces Ferry Road. Daddy buys bagels, lox, cream cheese, and pickled herring. He scrambles eggs with salami. After breakfast he and Mother read *The New York Times*. David and I look at the funnies in the Atlanta paper. I like Dondi, the war orphan. After the funnies, David and I wander around the house. There's never anything to do on Sunday.

Mother likes to go on Sunday drives. It's common for families to go on Sunday drives. Mother wants us to drive on small rural roads that pass little farms and little towns. Rural Georgia is beautiful. Poor but beautiful. In the car, Daddy listens to the ball game. I never know what teams are playing. Atlanta doesn't have a major league team. It only has a minor league baseball team called "The Crackers."

In the fall, we go to Georgia Tech football games. We take a thermos and a special football blanket in case it's chilly. We root for the Yellow Jackets. We sing "I'm a Ramblin' Wreck from Georgia Tech." We live in a universe of college football. It's the Bible Belt and the Football Belt.

On Sundays we sometimes go to the airport south of the city. The airport is a scenic destination. It's a showcase of aviation marvels and a place to relax. We sit on the observation deck and watch the planes take off and land. It's dreamy to watch the planes. Afterwards we dine at the airport's restaurant, a faux antebellum cabin for White diners. By the front door sits an old, cotton-haired Black man in a rocking chair. He pulls a bell cord to open and shut the door. Next to him is a basket for tips. When we leave, Daddy drops a dollar in the basket.

Even stranger is going to Aunt Fanny's Cabin. It's outside of Atlanta. There, young Black boys walk around with large chalkboard menus around their neck. And if you throw pennies, they dance. My family is liberal. We're against the Old South and segregation, yet we go to places that shout DIXIE!

Sunday is the worst day of the week. Sunday is a day

of war. All week there are skirmishes that climax on Sunday. Mother and Daddy fight and shout most of the day. To get Daddy's attention, Mother fights. If we go on a drive, there's often a fight. By late afternoon, the fighting winds down. We change into our best clothes and go to the club.

It's a Jewish club, one of three in Atlanta—the Mayfair, the Progressive, and the Standard. They're modeled after the restricted gentile clubs that don't allow Jews. At the club, we dine with Grandma and my Aunt Evelyn's family. I like to order shrimp cocktail and lamb chops. I like the frilly pastel paper hat that sits on the lamb chop's bone. The club's dining room is stuffy with heat in winter and frosty with air-conditioning in summer. If we go to the club to swim, or Daddy goes to play tennis, we eat hamburgers at the club's grill.

Best of all is to sit with Daddy at the club's bar, sipping a Shirley Temple and eating pistachios. The red shells stain my fingers. I have to be careful not to stain my Florence Eiseman dress. Sometimes there are big club events in the ballroom. Sometimes the ballroom is reserved for a birthday party or a Bar Mitzvah. In the club's lobby, Grandma plays the slot machines. She gives us nickels to play, too. I watch the rows of fruits and bells fly by. Before they stop, the rows quiver. It's like they're trying to decide whether we will win or lose. A row of three identical fruits or bells is a jackpot. Grandma loves to gamble. She and her friends play gin rummy and canasta for money. In Miami she goes to the races—horses and dogs. She laughs at everything and tells jokes. Grandma is a lot of fun.

Grandma was born Anna Aarons in New York. She was raised in Jewish Harlem. She's my only grandparent born in the US. Her father abandoned the family. She went to work as a secretary to support her mother and sisters. After she married Grandpa, she moved to Atlanta. Grandpa was no longer a peddler. He no longer went out into the countryside with a wagon and a mule. He had a store. From prosperous merchant, Grandpa became a wholesaler. Then he built Puritan Mills to manufacture feed and flour. Puritan Mills made him rich. Grandma was able to support her sisters and mother in New York with Grandpa's wealth.

Grandma's hair is dyed reddish brown. Her hair and eyes are almost the same color—a reddish fox. She wears nice dresses and nice shoes. She keeps up her appearance. I never met Grandma's mother. I'm told she dropped dead on the New York subway going to the beauty parlor.

Everyone in the family keeps up appearances except Daddy. Mother argues with Daddy to lose weight, fix his teeth, change his stained jacket or tie. She wants Daddy to make a good impression. Everyone knows that Daddy is very smart, but he doesn't make a good impression. Maybe it's indifference. Or depression. Maybe he has given up trying to please her. Or anyone.

My Aunt Evelyn's husband Joe is the opposite of Daddy. He wears expensive clothes—shirts, ties, shoes. He drives a sports car, first an Austin-Healey, then a Jaguar. He pays careful attention to how he looks. Uncle Joe is not a warm or friendly man, but he makes a good impression.

For years we eat together as a family at the club. Or at Ding Ho, the city's only Chinese restaurant, where they grow exotic vegetables on the roof of the building. We celebrate Jewish holidays together. And then it stops. We stop meeting at the club for Sunday dinner. We stop having Passover together. When my mother and my aunt stop speaking to each other, the family falls apart.

# 8

# TRAVELS

Grandma is a traveler. When Grandpa was alive, he and Grandma traveled everywhere. Wherever they went, she bought whatever she wanted—hand-painted china, Murano glass, gilded cages with mechanical birds that fluttered and sang, foreign dolls for my cousins and me. After they came home, crates would arrive with all the things she bought. On a postcard from Paris she wrote, *Drove by the Louvre today.* Everyone laughed at the message on the card. Even I knew why it was funny.

Every year they wintered in Miami Beach. Every year they went to Atlantic City to meet Grandma's sisters. Grandma always brought back bags of salt-water taffy. Yellow was my favorite flavor.

My parents are travelers, too. They often go to New York. Once they went to Mexico. There's a photo of them on a boat in the Floating Gardens of Xochimilco.

After Grandpa died, Grandma bought an apartment in Bal Harbour, a part of Miami Beach. She took cruises to the Far East, but she never got off the ship. She stayed on the ship to gamble and relax. When she returned home, she reported that the highlight of the cruise was her winning bingo scores.

At five I'm promised a trip to New York for my tenth

birthday. I count the years. Every year I remind my parents of their promise. In late spring of 1955, we fly to Idlewild Airport. Through the window of the taxi, I marvel at the skyscrapers and masses of people. Wherever I look, everything and everyone are pressed together. Daddy has told me that New York is the greatest city in the world. When I step out of the taxi, I feel a rush of the city's electricity. The feelings from my first trip to New York never leave me. Whenever I go there, I feel the same tremendous rush.

Daddy first went to New York when he was twelve. His father took him to see the Lindbergh parade. After his historic solo flight across the Atlantic, there was a giant tickertape parade to welcome Lindbergh home. A few months later, Daddy had his Bar Mitzvah. The next year he left home to enter college at UNC. By nineteen he had a Masters degree in Chemical Engineering. Daddy was precocious, but he also had exceptional teachers in high school. In Hendersonville where he lived, there were several sanitariums for tuberculosis. Before antibiotics, people came from all over for rest and fresh mountain air. Daddy's high school teachers were professors in other places. His Latin teacher taught Classics at the University of Chicago.

Daddy wants us to eat at Lindy's. Lindy's is a New York landmark. I ask if we can go to Dempsey's instead. I don't know why I'm crazy about Jack Dempsey. Maybe I read a book about him, or overheard Daddy say he was a great boxer. In his honor, I named my boxer puppy "Dempsey." A dozen years later, while visiting a friend in New York, I saw Jack Dempsey in a small grocery store on the Upper East Side. I poked my friend and said, "Isn't that Jack Dempsey?" I was surprised I recognized his old, rough and tough face. My friend was surprised, too.

In New York we stay at the Savoy Plaza. From the hotel window, I can look out at Central Park. I'd seen Broadway musicals on tour in Atlanta but not serious drama. My first real Broadway play is *The Desperate Hours* with Paul Newman. The play scares me more than I've ever been scared. I'm literally on the edge of my seat, watching a nightmare unfold on stage. I see how something *unreal* can be scariest of all. The next night we see *Damn Yankees*. It's about a devil, but it's not scary. It's a musical. Gwen Verdon is the star. She does a split that takes her from one side of the stage to the other.

We visit MOMA and the Bronx Zoo. We dine at Sardis and Toots Shor. We drop by an automat. We take a boat ride around Manhattan. Mother stays in New York to shop and visit art galleries. Daddy and I go by train to Washington.

I like riding trains. I like seeing fields and woods, kids waving and stations along the way. I'm happy to be alone with Daddy—except for one thing. He can see I'm worried. He asks what's wrong. I hesitate because I think I'll hurt Daddy's feelings. But then I say I'm worried about our hotel. A quizzical look passes over his face. What I don't say is I'm worried it won't be a nice hotel. Maybe it's because Daddy doesn't care about making money. Or because Mother says, "Your daddy can't make a dime." While some people call him a *genius*, geniuses are only smart in certain ways. Daddy is a loving parent, patient and kind. And he's a highly moral man. But I've been told I shouldn't rely on Daddy. With Mother it's worse. I can't rely on her for love or affection.

Our Washington hotel is The Mayflower. It's a lovely hotel. We visit the National Gallery, which Daddy calls The Mellon. I fall in love with the Impressionist painters. I go crazy over Renoir like I went crazy over Jack Dempsey. The next day Daddy has planned a visit to the Washington Monument. I tell him I don't care about monuments. I ask if we can go back to The Mellon. I explain that I've fallen in love with Renoir, Gauguin, Degas, and Monet. Daddy is pleased to skip the monuments. He loves paintings, too.

\*

That same year I have my stage debut at Atlanta's Theater Under the Stars. It starts with an audition where I sing "Oh, My Darling Clementine." I don't sing very well. I love to sing, but I'm nervous. Daddy asks if I can try again. The second time I do better. I'm selected to play one of the Siamese princesses in a summer-stock version of *The King and I*. I'm paid $25 for six performances. I'm fitted for a costume called a sarong. My skin is darkened with makeup. My hair is pinned inside a gold lamé donut on top of my head. I'm part of the professional cast. All the children sing. In one scene, we wave sheets of blue cloth for the river that "Little Liza" must cross to freedom. I have a speaking part. In my strong Southern accent, I make a speech that begs Anna to stay in Siam. *Dear friend and teacher, Do not go away. . . .* Despite my stage fright, I have a wonderful time.

For my future on Broadway, I'm not sure where to turn. I write to Mary Martin. I write ten careful, confidential pages about my admiration for her and my personal ambitions. In return, I get an impersonal form letter and an autographed photograph of her as Peter Pan. I'm inconsolable. I rip up the letter and photo. I thought Mary Martin would want to help.

# 9

# FIRST DEATH

Grandpa has tuberculosis. He has diabetes. He's senile, or nearly. He's moved from his home to Milledgeville. In Georgia if you want to say someone is crazy, all you have to say is "Milledgeville." That's enough. That's where the state hospital for the insane is located. Opened in 1842, it became the largest insane asylum in the world with 200 buildings on 2,000 acres. At its peak, there were 13,000 patients. A real horror show.

Grandpa is not at the state hospital. He's in a private sanitarium in Milledgeville. On the drive to see him, my cousin Nancy and I play Count the Cows. If there are more cows on your side of the car, you win unless there's a graveyard. A graveyard cancels out your cows. The tricky part is the other player has to see the graveyard. It's hard to count cows on one side and look for graveyards on the other.

When we visit Grandpa, he's on the porch of the sanitarium. He's in a rocking chair on the front porch. He looks like a very old child. His nose and head are round and doughy like a baby. His lapis blue eyes stare out with wonder and dismay. I'm not sure he recognizes us. He nods, but he doesn't talk or sing or tell jokes. He doesn't twist our cheeks or jiggle our chins or flap our lips with his fingers. It's sad to see Grandpa so subdued. When we leave, I know I'll never see him again.

Nancy and I are allowed to go to Grandpa's funeral. Mother tells me I can go, but I can't wear black. "Children don't wear black," she says. It must be bad luck for children to wear black. Mother is filled with superstitions to safeguard us from bad luck. She makes us knock on wood and chew thread. And yet no matter what, she says she's unlucky. She says we're all unlucky.

The funeral overflows from the chapel to the lawn. "The city of Atlanta loved your grandfather," Mother says. He was the first Ashkenazi Jew invited to join The Temple and the Standard Club. Mother boasts of these achievements because The Temple and Standard Club were established for wealthy German Jews. There's a hierarchy of status between German and Ashkenazi Jews.

Mother believes that Grandpa loved her more than her sisters. All three sisters are beautiful, but only my mother has blue eyes like him. Large and blue like stones under the sea. She thinks he loved her most because of her eyes. She thinks he proved that she was his favorite by bringing her a splendid coat. I think it's because she almost died as a child. She caught a chill that turned into pneumonia. From pneumonia her condition worsened to empyema. The doctors said it was hopeless. The doctors brought stuffed animals to the hospital because they thought she would die.

Mother has an indentation on the side of her chest. The indentation is where the pus was drained from her left lung. The surgery probably saved her, but she had to lie on one side for a year, which paralyzed her arm. To bring the arm back to life, a nurse massaged it in scalding water. She said the scalding water was the hardest part—harder than lying on her side and harder than surgery.

Mother stayed in bed for three years. She missed kindergarten and first grade. As a result of the surgery, her left breast is shriveled. She wears a soft molded piece of foam called a "falsie" inside the left cup of her brassiere. Before I have breasts, I think mine will be lopsided like hers.

Although Grandpa was a member of The Temple, he preferred Ahavath Achim. The Temple is reform. Ahavath Achim is conservative. Grandpa preferred the traditions of a cantor and services in Hebrew. Although I go to Sunday school at The Temple, on the High Holidays our family goes to both The Temple and Ahavath Achim. At Ahavath Achim, we sit in a row of seats reserved for the Abelman family. The row has a plaque with Grandpa's name. He donated a large sum to the synagogue's new building so our row of seats is at the front.

I long for a connection to God, but I don't find it at The Temple or Ahavath Achim. I sometimes sing "Jesus Loves Me." I sing it on the school bus with my gentile friends. I sing it at home. When I sing it, Daddy laughs.

He think it's funny to hear me sing a song about Jesus. He's an atheist. He believes in nothing, but I desperately want to believe in something. When I sing "Jesus Loves Me," Mother never laughs. "That's a tacky song," Mother says.

In 1958 our synagogue is bombed. There's a big hole in The Temple's sanctuary. Through the hole you can see the highway. Some say The Temple was bombed because Rabbi Rothschild is a friend of Dr. King's. Others say the bomber made a mistake and meant to destroy a *Jewier* synagogue. The day after the bombing, we go to services. Daddy goes. He's proud to go. Under the circumstances, he's proud to be a Jew. We have to walk through a police line to get inside the sanctuary. It's a beautiful sanctuary with a beautiful domed ceiling and stained glass windows. I listen to Rabbi Rothschild. I hear the sadness and anger in his words. Through them I feel part of an ancient tribe.

There's a Southern tradition that Mother practices like a religion. It's called TL, which translates as *trade last*. I've never heard of this game except in the South. I'm not sure if it's played anywhere else. I doubt men play it. It's a petty game of flattery. I think it's a game that only women play. It has one rule—if so-and-so hears a compliment about you, you must first tell so-and-so a compliment you heard about them. Not your own opinion but something someone else has said.

"I have a TL for you." That's how the game begins.

Mother often has a TL for me. I'm sure she's sick of hearing people say nice things about me. Instead, she wants to hear nice things about herself. However, I rarely talk to grownups at the club or The Temple. If I do, it's only to exchange niceties. *Hello, how are you? Fine. How are you?* It's unrealistic to think that an adult is going to comment to me about Mother's eyes, or clothes, or wit. I'm sometimes forced to invent a TL. Or repeat something I heard before. If I say I don't care about a TL, Mother gets angry.

She also interrogates me about other women. She asks my opinion of Sonia, Mitzi, Barbara, and her sister Evelyn. "Do you think she's attractive?" she asks. "Do you think she's more attractive than me?" If I admit one of them is pretty, she gets angry. She points out their physical flaws. Or dopey personalities. She says, "Your father likes *her*." Then she puts down his cheap hillbilly taste.

Daddy hates snobbery. He hates the word *cheap*. He talks to everyone. He talks to men at filling stations, waitresses in restaurants, bellhops at hotels. He doesn't say, "Fill it up!" He doesn't order people around but converses with them. Daddy is an egalitarian. But his friendliness annoys Mother. For Mother talking to these people is a waste of time. She has no patience for Daddy's conviviality, especially with working-class strangers. She doesn't talk to everyone. In fact, she hardly talks to anyone. She doesn't have the interest. Most people are beneath her. Most people aren't worth the effort.

On a hellishly hot afternoon, Daddy and I ride by a tenement house. Outside the tenement, women are seated on the front stoop. They're smoking and fanning themselves with rolled newspapers. They're watching their babies run around in diapers and play in the dirt yard.

"It's a waste for them to smoke," I say to impress Daddy. I'm young, maybe ten or eleven. I want Daddy to think I'm observant. I want him to commend me for my observations. "They should save their money for their kids," I say.

Daddy doesn't say anything. He's thinking and smoking. Finally, he says, "A cigarette might be the only pleasure they have today."

His tone is hurtful. His tone puts me down. He wants to make sure I don't think I'm better than they are. He doesn't want me to be judgmental or grow up to be a snob. After I get over my hurt, I realize Daddy is right. His words affect me deeply. His words help me see that small pleasures explain a lot about life. Everybody needs small pleasures. Even without money, there are ways to have them. Sitting, smoking, talking to friends, watching kids—these are pleasures almost anyone can enjoy.

After Grandpa dies, Daddy leaves Puritan Mills. He starts his own business—promoting and selling hydroponic grass-growing machines. These machines reduce the need for pasture land. The grass from these machines reduces the amount of radiation in milk. Milk from cows who eat hydroponic grass is healthier. Kids who drink the milk are healthier. That's the pitch. Daddy works with a scientist at Georgia Tech. They exhibit the grass-growing machines at the state fair. They try to interest farmers in growing grass in large hydroponic boxes. Maybe it's a quirky idea, or ahead of its time. It's probably exciting for Daddy to do something brainy. In the end, grass-growing machines are a flop.

Daddy tries roofing and siding. He stays in his office in Atlanta while salesmen go out to farms and small towns. The salesmen hustle folks into fixing up their houses. They're flashy dressers and fast talkers. They fast-talk poor people into buying new roofs and metal siding. They show them scrapbooks—before and after. They cut deals. It's a crummy business.

Uncle Joe has turned part of Puritan Mills into a successful home-supply business. Uncle Joe is a successful businessman. But Daddy has no business sense. His brilliance doesn't add up to anything practical. It doesn't pay the bills. Daddy is going downhill. He doesn't like his work, and his marriage is unhappy.

Mother attacks him for his failings, but she isn't deprived. She has her own money. She has money from Puritan Mills to spend on cars, trips, and clothes. She drives a Packard Caribbean with sterling silver keys. The glove compartment has a sterling silver plaque with her name engraved on it. She trades the Packard for a Mercedes-Benz. No one in Atlanta drives a Mercedes.

She's the first. Daddy's sister Bessie worked in a factory during the war. Bessie doesn't approve of Jews buying anything German. Daddy drives my grandmother's cast-off Cadillacs. When he buys a new car, it's a Rambler. The most unpretentious car on the road.

My parents are two extremes. Mother is artistic and materialistic. Daddy is intellectual and indifferent to the material world. He cares about ideas and politics. He teaches political science at a night school for adults. He's trying to write a murder mystery about the realtor who was killed in my aunt's basement.

But Daddy has a big problem. When he's home, he drinks all the time. When he and Mother go out to restaurants or the club with friends on Saturday night, they argue on Sunday about how much he drinks. Mother says none of their friends will go out with them because he drinks. At home he watches TV—*idiot box*, he calls it. He falls off the couch. He sleepwalks. He's a lively, funny, warm, gregarious man, but underneath the good humor and warmth, there's something wrong.

Daddy has to be pushed to get angry. Mother pushes him to get angry. When he's angry, he says things that make Mother feel stupid. As I get older, I learn to make her feel stupid, too. I imitate Daddy. If Mother blows hot, Daddy and I blow cold and distant.

"I can't have a relationship with you and your father," Mother says.

On weekends I try to escape. I go to my cousin

Nancy's house, or my friend Ellen's. At Ellen's house the dinners are proper with several courses, cooked by one woman and served by another. One night artichokes are the first course. Ellen shows me how to pull off the leaves and dip the ends into a silver bowl with lemon butter. When I tell Mother that I ate my first artichoke, she says, "Don't be ridiculous! Of course, you've eaten an artichoke!" She asks if I told Ellen's family that I went to Europe, instead of pretending I never ate an artichoke.

My first rock concert is at Lakewood Speedway. A friend's mother drives us. It's in the afternoon, safe and sanitary. We sit by the racetrack in the grandstand. We clap and sing along to The Big Bopper and Conway Twitty. Buddy Holly is the headliner. We all love Buddy Holly—his goofy looks and twangy voice that disguise his heartbreak and pain. Our seventh-grade teacher Mrs. Banks plays Buddy Holly records and lets us dance. We get to dance almost every afternoon. After we push the desks to the side, the whole class does The Stroll. It's a sad day when The Big Bopper (29), Buddy Holly (22), and Richie Valens (17) are killed in a plane crash. They're famous singers, but their young deaths feel personal.

Ellen and I live in our own little universe, both Jewish girls with few neighbors or playmates, both studious and well-behaved. We share a lot, but I have thoughts and feelings that I hardly understand. Philosophical thoughts and emotional feelings. I'm looking for a guide to the future.

Then I make a fantastic discovery. At twelve I discover that life has two basic paths—either freedom or happiness. One or the other, and you have to choose. I can see that my idea of happiness will require compromise. That's why, if given a choice, I'd rather be free.

I wonder who else has these kinds of dilemmas. When I describe them to Ellen, she listens. But I don't think she understands. I don't think she thinks about the same things. I'm alone after all.

## 10

## LIFE AQUATIC

Jekyll Island is a wilderness of empty beaches, forests full of deer and other creatures, oaks draped in Spanish moss, and nesting sites for birds and loggerhead turtles. Over the sea channels, shrimp boats spread their nets like wings. It's an enchanted place with no hotels and few new houses. At one end of the island are shuttered mansions. Called "cottages" by the members of the Jekyll Island Club, they were built in the late nineteenth century by the wealthiest men in the world (Rockefeller, Morgan, Vanderbilt, Pulitzer, et al.). Before air travel, these families yachted south in winter to hunt and fish on the island.

Mother and Aunt Evelyn rent a house on Jekyll Island. They rent it from friends in Atlanta. It's a ranch-style house with a wooden exterior and sliding glass doors, big enough for two families. During our first week, Mother wakes us at dawn. We walk to the beach in the gauzy light. There, we see the giant turtles. They've emerged from the surf and have started to climb to the dunes. Slowly, they inch their way over the sand. The churning ocean, the fiery sunrise, the ancient reptiles—I've never seen anything so beautiful and terrifying.

We watch the turtles dig their nests with their

flippers. Then they settle on the nests to lay their eggs. Their grunts make it sound painful, but maybe I'm mistaken. After this monumental effort, they cover the nests with sand and inch their way back to the sea.

A ranger stands by to protect the eggs from poachers. He tells us that turtle eggs are very valuable. That's why poachers come to steal the eggs. He tells us that each turtle lays approximately a hundred eggs. After they hatch, most will be eaten by birds. In their dash to the shoreline, they're easy prey. Others will be eaten by fish. Only a few will survive.

*Is this the Creator's plan?* passes through my mind. The effort, the slaughter, the futility. "They die before they live," I cry.

"For God's sake," Mother says. "If you're going to cry over baby turtles, you'll cry about everything for the rest of your life."

And she's right. Baby roosters and baby turtles, one death manufactured, the other a fact of nature. I'm raw, and Mother is as hard as a nut.

Days pass on the island at the beach or the fishing pier. We swim. We build sand castles. We collect seashells. On rainy days, we play cards and board games. At the bait shop, my cousins and I buy a bag of chicken necks. There's nothing more disgusting than a raw chicken neck. But I make myself pull one out from the bloody bag. Then I put the neck inside a wire crab trap. Once the trap doors are shut, we hang the baskets off the pier.

Then we wait. It's not long before the crabs crawl in the traps and can't crawl out. Soon there are enough crabs for dinner.

We only go to Jekyll Island one time. It's a nearly abandoned island. Usually, we go to St. Simon's. It's also an island with motels, restaurants, miniature golf, and tourists. It's fun, but it's not enchanted.

Mother persuades Daddy to drive us to Sea Island. We ride over the drawbridges that link the islands. I crank down the window to feel warm rain on my arm. I crank up the window so I don't smell the stinky paper mill or low tide.

On Sea Island, Daddy circles around the streets of large stucco homes. Homes with wrought-iron balconies and mowed green lawns. Mother asks Daddy to stop at The Cloister. The Cloister is the reason we've come to Sea Island. The Cloister is a luxury hotel—and *restricted*. The entire island is restricted. Jews are banned from renting or buying houses, or staying at The Cloister. My grandparents were refused a reservation. Mother is angry we can't stay on Sea Island. Daddy says we shouldn't care about going places where we're not welcome. Mother says Jews should be allowed to go anywhere. A few years later, when a high school friend invites me to vacation with her family on Sea Island, Daddy doesn't let me go.

The storms at the beach are huge. The ocean boils. The sky turns inky black. It's as if a genie has filled the whole sky. Outside, I run around drunk on air. I run until lightning rips the sky open. As soon as I see lightning,

I count. I wait for the crash of thunder. I calculate the distance between the lightning and the thunder. If they're almost simultaneous, I rush inside. Some kids are afraid of thunder. They hide from thunder under the bed. But thunder won't hurt me. It's only lightning that's dangerous. It's why we have a lightning rod attached to the roof of our house.

Aunt Tillie has a house at Myrtle Beach. Aunt Tillie is Uncle Julius' mother. Technically, we're not related. Technically, Julius is married to Daddy's sister Bessie. But Aunt Tillie makes everyone feel like family. When she bought the beach house, she reported that it had two views of the ocean. When asked how, she explained that a hotel was directly across the street. "You can see the ocean on either side of the hotel," Aunt Tillie said. She's a continuous source of amusement.

Ten of us fill Aunt Tillie's clapboard house. The rooms smell like wet towels. Sand crunches on the bare floors. No matter how much I shower and shake, sand gets in my sheets. My cousin Gail and I sleep on the screen porch. The house is far from the hubbub of the amusement park, the tourist shops, the restaurants, and miniature golf. Mostly, we enjoy the beach.

Uncle Julius loves to fish. He shows us how to hook worms. A worm is not as ugly as a chicken neck, but it's a wriggling, living thing. Despite my squeamishness, I quickly become an expert—picking worms out of a bucket and jabbing them with a hook.

When we're not on vacation, we're at the club pool.

On weekdays only women and children are at the club. On weekends men with hairy chests and hairy legs lie beside their wives on chaise lounges. If their legs are splayed, I look up inside their swim trunks. I look at the bulges in the mesh sack of their swim trunks. When I was little, I used to shower with Daddy. I used to stand between his hairy legs.

On hot summer nights, we stop at Fred's Fruit Emporium. Fred's is a fruit market with a large screened porch. At Fred's we sit at a picnic table and eat watermelon. We love Georgia watermelon. The best watermelons grow in Georgia. The watermelon is so sweet that we sprinkle it with salt. We eat the pink spongy wedges down to the rind. Outside the screened porch, lightning bugs fly around. They look like electric watermelon seeds.

# 11

# ABROAD

It's seventeen hours to fly from New York to London. We stop in Greenland to refuel. We stop in Shannon to shop. Mother and I are on a two-week, five-country tour of Europe with a dozen Atlanta couples—middle-aged and prosperous. Mother and I are the only Jews. I'm the only child. I'm barely thirteen, not so young or old, somewhere in between. I'm here because Daddy didn't want to go. I'm not sure why. Maybe he saw enough of Europe during the war.

The tour officially begins in London. We visit Westminster Abbey. We visit the Tower and learn about the murder of the young royal princes. We see the Crown Jewels. We see the Changing of the Guard. At Madame Tussauds Wax Museum, my favorite is Sleeping Beauty. She lies in a satin-lined coffin. Her wax breast rises and falls to a hidden recording of every breath. Mother and I sneak away from the tour to shop at Harrods and eat at The Savoy. Wherever Mother goes, she eats at the most famous restaurants. Wherever we go, men admire her. In her gray gaberdine suit with the gray fox collar, they admire her. They think she's my older sister. As I said, Mother dresses like a movie star.

In Brussels we visit the World's Fair. The USSR and

the US compete for the biggest pavilions—impressive monuments versus the gadgets of daily American life. We leave Brussels and travel on a tour bus. We ride along the Rhine with river barges beside us and castles on hillsides above us. They look like quaint illustrations from a book of fairy tales. In Cologne there are still ruins from the war. In Heidelberg we lunch at the Red Ox Inn. Students' names are carved on old tables from other centuries. Everything we see is from the past. The past is a living thing. Art is a living thing. We're surrounded by statues and paintings. For souvenirs I buy cloisonné charms, each with the name and symbol of a city or town.

Outside Bern, our hotel is a chalet with fields of wild flowers and Alpine peaks covered with snow. More illustrations from one of my favorite books, *Heidi*. Like her I scamper around the mountainside. I ride the funicular up the mountain. For meals there's fondue and lots of chocolate.

On the morning of our departure, I see my mother scrunched over our bathroom sink. She has managed to unscrew the two sink handles. Brass and porcelain etched with *Froid* and *Chaud*. She tells me they'll go in our fancy powder room at home. The powder room has silver leaf wallpaper and a large oval mirror swagged with crystal rope. The sink handles will make it fancier.

I know the minute difference between taking, borrowing, lending, and stealing. I know the difference between right and wrong. But in defense of Mother, I rationalize. I assume she has asked permission. Or confirmed that the sink handles are worthless. Or already arranged to buy them.

I carry our suitcases downstairs to the bus. The luggage hatch is propped up. The bus is idling. The other passengers are in their seats. Mother arrives last. The bus door slams shut. The mammoth machine slowly rolls over the gravel towards the road.

"Stop! Stop!" It's the stout Swiss concierge running after us. He's waving his arms like windmills and shouting, "Stop! Stop!"

He confers with our tour guide. In turn, the guide informs us that two sink handles are missing from one of our rooms. An oceanic hum fills the air. The others know they aren't thieves. Or lunatics. Poor Mother! She waits. Everyone waits. We can't leave until the handles are returned. Finally, she gropes inside her purse. She hesitates. She rummages around. She pretends. And then with feigned surprise, she pulls out the missing handles. And passes them to the front of the bus.

Loud enough for everyone to hear, Mother asks me, "Can you tell us why you took them?"

I shut my eyes, wishing to be whisked away to the mountaintop. Wishing I could spend my life with Heidi, Grandfather, and the goats. When my eyes open, nothing has changed. Since I saw her take them, I must be partly to blame. However, I am certain of two things. First, no one believes a child would steal bathroom fixtures. And second, my innocence doesn't matter. What matters is an explanation, reasonable or not. Every misdeed needs a scapegoat. Mother can't admit her guilt so I am blamed in her stead. I accept my sentence. I don't say a word in my defense. I rise from my seat and go to the back of the bus where I burn with shame.

Paris is our last stop. Outside our hotel, there are mass protests in the street. Thousands are marching in protest. It's the Algerian crisis. As a result, we are forced to change hotels. One night Mother wants to leave me alone. But I'm afraid. I'm afraid of the protestors. I'm afraid the hotel will be bombed. I beg Mother to take me with her.

At the Folies Bergère, Mother blocks my face with her hand. "Close your eyes," she says.

I can see through her fingers. The gorgeous dancers are barely clothed. Soon I become accustomed to watching them. More interesting than their glamorous headdresses and the elaborate productions is my realization that this is their job. Dancing naked looks fun—and it's a job!

# 12

# WAR STORIES AND V-MAIL

Batesburg is a small town in the sand hills of South Carolina where Aunt Bessie and Uncle Julius live. They own a department store called Garber's, one of a small chain owned by Uncle Julius and his brothers. On Saturdays country folk come to town to shop. During harvest season, the store stays open until midnight. On busy weekends my cousins Gail and Ronnie work in the store.

For Thanksgiving we always go to Batesburg. The weekend alternates between family feasts and college football. In the large, pleasant den, we flop on two long couches to watch the Bowl games. Or the kids play in the giant backyard under the giant pecan trees. It's a comfortable house. David and I are always comfortable at Bessie's. There are no fights or bad behavior or drama. These are the most normal people I know.

The railroad tracks are close to the house, only a few doors away. Day and night, we hear the trains. Sometimes we put a penny on the track and go back later to find it smashed. To walk to downtown, we have to cross the railroad tracks. Garber's is the town's largest store. It sells every kind of clothing for every age. The racks of clothes are packed tightly together. Everything smells of sizing and dust. Sunlight streaks through the front windows, and the wooden floors creak. David and I pick out new socks, new shoes, and new underwear at Garber's. Aunt Bessie tells us to help ourselves to whatever we need.

Twice a year, Bessie and Julius go to New York. They shop at the wholesale showrooms in New York's Garment District. They select items to sell at Garber's for the next season. They mostly sell modestly priced clothing, but there are also specialty items.

"Only country people shop at Garber's," Mother says. But occasionally, she shops there, too. She asks Bessie to buy her a Pauline Trigère coat. It's a very expensive coat that Bessie can get wholesale. One Pauline Trigère coat is shipped to Garber's.

Uncle Julius was born in Batesburg, in the house where his mother lives. His mother is Aunt Tillie. Her house is a large white Victorian with glossy black trim and a porch that wraps around the front and side. It's a warren of bedrooms and baths. Since Uncle Julius and Aunt Bessie live next door, I visit Aunt Tilly at her house. Its interior is dark and cool, the window shades pulled down—a house preserved from another age.

Whenever Uncle Julius talks about his mother, he laughs. He has a high, innocent laugh, almost a giggle. It's a contagious laugh. Whenever I hear it, I laugh, too. Uncle Julius must have had this laugh since he was a boy. I think his laugh means that he had a happy childhood.

There are only a few Jews in Batesburg. My aunt and uncle and their kids plus Julius' sister Sarah, her husband Sam Bogo, and their daughter Phyllis. Sam Bogo owns the movie theater, so we never have to pay.

Daddy and Uncle Julius were together in the Navy. They were Naval officers and old friends. When Daddy's ship arrived on a Pacific island, the Seabees were all drunk. The Seabees arrived first to prepare the island for the Navy's landing. The Seabees found a cache of Japanese beer and camouflaged it. They buried and marked it—EXTREME DANGER! Daddy persuaded them to reveal the location of the beer. Then he got drunk, too.

War letters were called V-mail. Tissue-thin blue paper folded up to make an envelope. At home there's a box of V-mail from Daddy to Mother. Each piece of V-mail had to be read by a censor. If the censor objected to anything, the words were blacked out.

Daddy wrote Mother a joke letter he redacted himself.

*DEAREST RITA,*
*I AM IN _____*
*AND SOON WILL BE MEETING _____*
*ALMOST AS BEAUTIFUL AS YOU*
*THE TWO OF US WILL TRAVEL TO _____*
*AND BE AWAY FOR _____*
*IT'S A SPECIAL MISSION FOR _____*
*DON'T LET THIS WORRY YOU*
*FAITHFULLY YOURS, EDDIE*

Daddy was a scientist. Before the war, he worked as a research chemist. For the Navy, he invented something to do with depth charges. There's a training film that Daddy made with the actor Eddie Albert. The film trained admirals on how to use these depth charges. Daddy said that US depth charges killed more Americans than Germans.

During the war, Daddy wrote up the heroic exploits of a fictional sailor. Throughout the war, he submitted descriptions of his hero's acts of bravery. Finally, the War Department took notice. They gave the sailor a medal. Daddy's stories made war sound ludicrous. Tragic but ludicrous.

Mother was also a prankster. When she and Daddy first married, they lived near Asheville in the mountains of North Carolina. Daddy worked for The American Enka Company near Asheville. As a joke, Mother used to send flowers to herself from "a secret admirer." Or she signed the card from "the village idiot." It was a joke she played on Daddy.

Enka fabricated rayon. During the war, they produced fabric for parachutes. Enka claimed that Daddy's job was "classified." Daddy said their claim of "classified" was false. He took Enka to court to release him from his contract. After Daddy won the case, he joined the Navy. Mother and Daddy moved from Asheville to Washington. They lived in the Georgetown section of Washington.

However, Daddy traveled a great deal. He was on ships in the Atlantic and Pacific. He was in London during the Blitz.

I never witnessed it, but I love to imagine their humor and happiness together. Reading Daddy's V-mail helps me believe that he and Mother used to be in love.

## 13

## OUT AND ABOUT

Sometimes Nancy and I skip the matinee at the Buckhead theater. Instead, we catch the bus to downtown Atlanta. Each bus marked with WHITE FORWARD, COLORED REAR. Even when the rear is crowded and the front empty, there's an invisible line that Black people can't cross. This line is the first one I discover in a world of invisible lines.

On Saturdays the buses are mostly empty. We ride along Peachtree Road, broad and lined with large churches and shade trees. We pass Garden Hills, an enclave of houses and apartment buildings with a movie theater. Grandma took me there to see *The Red Shoes*. It made an impression that never went away, not unlike the impression of the drowning sisters who wanted to swim the English Channel.

At Fred's Fruit Emporium, there's a long dip followed by a long incline with apartment buildings and forlorn shops. These city blocks feel abandoned. Like certain places in all cities, there's a feeling of emptiness. The Luau restaurant and Piedmont Hospital are followed by Brookwood Station, The Temple, and more churches.

At Pershing Point, Peachtree Road divides into Peachtree Street and West Peachtree Street. The bus continues past the elegant oasis of the High Art Museum and the entrance to Ansley Park. Past Tenth Street's seedy bars and rooming houses. Past the fashionable Georgian Terrace Hotel and the Fox Theater. The Fox is designed like a mosque with minarets, mosaics, and ceilings that twinkle with stars. When we reach downtown, it's an eddy of energy. The sidewalks overflow with Black women in stylish dresses, high heels, and hats.

Nancy and I race off the bus to Woolworth's counter for grilled cheese sandwiches and fountain Cokes. We wander around Davison's lingerie department, fondling negligees. Farther downtown are movie theaters, hotels, restaurants, and the white marble Carnegie Library fronted by Ionic columns. The trick store is my favorite stop. I usually buy a trick or two to play on an unsuspecting relative. Mr. Peanut strolls by with a peanut head and peanut torso, a top hat and cane. Mr. Peanut is an ambulatory ad for Planter's Peanuts. Raw, roasted, boiled, salted, unsalted, everybody loves peanuts.

If we stay in Buckhead, David often comes with us to the movies. I buy him treats. I introduce him to my friends. David is nervous. He talks too much. He doesn't know how to behave. He's hard to understand. I have to explain what he says.

Mother never invites David's classmates to our house. The children at his school have various afflictions. Afflictions that Mother considers inferior to David. She doesn't want them associated with David. He never gets to have a friend his own age. That's why my friends are important. He has a crush on my friend Lynn. She's pretty and petite. And just David's size.

I wish David were normal. I wish he didn't stand out. No one else has to take their brother to the movies. I'm the only one.

"He's smarter than your dumb cousins," Mother says.

At home Mother sometimes plays with us. She gets down on the carpet. David and I get down on the carpet with her. She imitates a dog. She wags her backside and barks. She imitates a monkey. She sticks her tongue inside her cheek and scratches her armpit. She screeches like a monkey. She's a great mimic. It's fun to play with her. But it's also scary. Mother is unpredictable. She frightens us. She frightens everyone.

## 14

## SEX EDUCATION

David and I were once variations of the same theme—odd, graceless children bound to each other by our parents. But now we're breaking apart. I'm going in one direction, towards sociability. David is going in another, towards further isolation.

Westminster, my new high school, looks like a college. It sits on forty acres of woods and fields with stately, white-columned brick buildings. It's a Protestant school that requires mandatory Bible study and attendance at religious services. We read the King James, Genesis to Revelations. There are three Jewish girls and one Catholic in my class. I have to study in earnest.

All week I hide in my room to study. As soon as I finish, I talk on my Princess phone and listen to soul music on the radio. I talk to boys and girls. Sometimes we talk for hours. The radio and phone lessen my sense of banishment. I live in a cold, isolated corner of a cold, isolated house.

Winter is worse than other seasons. Winter is when it's literally cold. Two furnaces are inadequate. Blankets and down comforters are inadequate. The casement windows leak cold air, and outside the leafless branches move in menacing ways.

Things deteriorate further with Mother. If I contradict her, she curses me. She digs her fingernails into my arms and scratches me. When she attacks, I try to put up a shield. I try to steel myself and pretend she can't hurt me. I've trained myself to act cool and indifferent. But her meanness breaks me down. I hate her when she breaks me down. I run to my room and sob until I'm dry. I'm so dry I can't make tears. Sometimes I think I must love her very much for her to break me down. After I've sobbed for a long time, she breaks down, too.

"I'm sorry, I didn't mean to hurt you," she says.

She wants me to forgive her. She begs me to forgive her. She needs my forgiveness. She apologizes and believes it's over. Once I say everything is okay, she can forget what happened. She can think it's behind us. She doesn't see her poison left inside me.

Boys never thought I was attractive. They thought I was gawky. I'm not gawky anymore. I don't try to impress boys with intelligence. I try to impress them with charm. Especially older boys with cars. They have to have a car because I live far from town. They pick me up and take me out. We go to dinner, movies, dances. Chuck Berry, Bo Diddley, Doug Clark and the Hot Nuts, Ray Charles headline at the ballrooms in the White hotels. We dance for hours. When we aren't dancing, we're flirting. The boys are drinking and telling dirty jokes. I don't drink. I don't like how alcohol affects me—and everyone around me. Maybe I take a swig from my parents' bottle of Drambuie, or sip G&T on a hot day. But I get dizzy if I drink. I'm afraid I might lose control.

Date nights usually end with parking. Either on a dark street or a place called Fog Island. Fog Island is the unofficial name for a stretch of residential road with ground fog. It's a parking lot for teenage sex. With the car lights off, you disappear in Fog Island. Boys try to go to first base, second base, third base, and all the way home. They coax me around the bases. First and second are fine. I like to be kissed. I like to be gnawed and pawed. I let them put their tongue in my mouth. I let them rub my breasts. I let them hump me. But I don't go all the way. I have no desire to go all the way. *All the way* sounds like there's something to lose. I'm not ready to lose anything.

When Mother gets mad, she calls me a *slut*. I laugh when she calls me a slut. In fact, I like the word. I like its percussive sound. I like its suggestiveness. But in truth, I'm inexperienced and naive. I was once a sensual little girl—happily running naked around the yard. Puberty changed me into a prude. Mother says I should have a curfew. Daddy disagrees. He says there's nothing I can do after a curfew that I can't do before. Daddy asks me if I need birth control. When I first heard the term, I thought it meant a law that restricted the number of kids you could have. But when Daddy asks me, he means something else. I know what he means. It's an embarrassing question. I don't want him to ask these kinds of questions. I don't want him to think I'm going all the way. Or hope I'm going all the way. I think it's inappropriate for him to ask. I think Daddy is too free.

Tim grew up in Los Angeles. Now he goes to military school in Atlanta. He misses California. He misses surfing. When he gets out of school, he's going to surf around the world. Tim is the only boy I know who wants to be a bum. I find that alluring. I think it's a form of being free. Or maybe it's because Mother calls Daddy a bum. She thinks he's the smartest man alive—but a bum.

On weekends Tim comes to our house. From our house, he calls his father in Hollywood. He uses our phone to call long distance. Tim calls a dozen different bars on Sunset Boulevard where his father might be. He calls until he reaches him. I sometimes talk to his father in a bar in Hollywood. It's like talking to a dream.

Tim's mother is the movie star Susan Hayward. After she divorced Tim's father, she married a wealthy man from Georgia. She left Hollywood to live on a farm. Tim invites me to visit his mother's farm outside Carollton. Tim's twin brother comes and brings a girlfriend, too. The twins are different. Tim's brother doesn't want to be a surfer. He wants to be a vet. Susan Hayward fixes us fried chicken and coleslaw for lunch. She brings the platters of food to a picnic table outside. She stands beside the table and chats with us while we eat. Dressed in a purple gingham blouse and matching pedal-pushers, she's very casual. But she's also Susan Hayward, famous for her halo of red hair, her beautiful, hypnotic voice, and her pale white skin. Talking to her is also like a dream. Before we leave, Tim lets me hold her Oscar.

A late date is when one boy drops you off at a respectable hour so your parents think you're safely home—and another boy picks you up. Late dates are impossible at my house. If I want to make a late date, I have to spend the night at Nancy's house. Her house makes late dating very convenient. It has an outside door off her brother Larry's room. Late dates are exciting, but there's nowhere to go. Everything is closed. Movie theaters, restaurants, clubs are closed. We can only go to a golf course or a park. Nights on an empty golf course are magical. The smell of mowed grass, the warm air with fresh cool pockets, the silvery lawns, the deep blue-black sky, the enchanting fireflies are magic.

In summers I date lifeguards who work at the Standard Club. The Standard Club is a Jewish club, but the lifeguards are gentile. On a date with a lifeguard, we get arrested at a private lake on Roswell Road. Lots of teenagers know about this lake. Trespassing is a problem for the lake's owners. We get arrested because the owners have called the police. There are four of us. Three are in college and over eighteen. I'm in high school and sixteen. When the police arrive, they charge us with disturbing the peace instead of trespassing. We aren't disturbing the peace, but we're grateful for the downgrade. Disturbing the peace is a misdemeanor. Trespassing requires a hearing before a grand jury.

When the police ask my age, I lie. "Eighteen," I say.

Because of the police, it's extremely late when I get home. Mother is at the front door. She's standing at the front door in her fur coat and pajamas.

"Where have you been?" She screams at me. "Do you know what time it is?" She screams at my date.

I'm wearing a bathing suit and my date's shirt. "We were at a wedding reception," I say cooly. "They got married at a pool."

It's an absurd lie, but Mother doesn't dispute it. It's easy to lie. I just lied to the police. It's easy to lie to Mother.

I receive a summons by mail. There's a date when I have to appear in court. There's a downtown courtroom where I have to go. The four of us wait for hours in the courtroom. We wait for the judge to hear our case. We listen as the judge hears dozens of other misdemeanor cases—shoplifting, prostitution, gambling. Each suspect is Black. Man, woman, young, old, each is fined *and* sentenced to jail. The longer we wait and listen, the more we panic. When it's our turn, the judge asks where we go to school. We go to Duke, the University of Georgia, UNC, and my high school Westminster. The judge dismisses the charges. We are White and free to go.

A week later, the court clerk calls my house. When he

introduces himself, I think he must be calling because I lied about my age. I think he's going to order me back to court. But I'm mistaken. He wants to ask me on a date. I tell him how old I really am. I worry he might report me, but I quickly realize he'd get in trouble for calling. My lie is safe.

## 15

# TREE OF KNOWLEDGE

Before my parents separate, my mother is almost always mad at people and things, animate and inanimate—her sisters, salesclerks, her mother, traffic lights, appliances, David, me, and most of all, Daddy. If a fight is especially bad, Daddy walks out. He gets in his car and leaves. I think fighting is Mother's way of getting his attention, but it's a futile strategy. She's a fighter, and he's a pacifist. Daddy likes to say, "Peace at any price."

When Daddy leaves, he spends the night at my aunt's house. My Aunt Evelyn has a guest room where he can spend the night. Mother says that her sister is in love with Daddy. She says that her sister tries to monopolize Daddy. Aunt Evelyn has intellectual interests with no one to talk to except Daddy. Daddy makes her feel clever. She makes Daddy feel needed. I'm sure they commiserate about Mother. Whatever their relationship, it drives my mother crazy. She and my aunt fight over Daddy. They fight publicly. At the club, Mother once threw a drink on my aunt. At home she accuses Daddy of *screwing* her sister. Every time they fight, she accuses Daddy of having an affair. It makes me sad, but I try not to engage. I try to believe their marriage is not my problem.

When they separate, it's a relief. We leave the big,

gloomy house on Northside Drive. David and I move with Mother to a beautiful three-bedroom apartment at the corner of Peachtree and 15th Street. There's an elevator, an elevator man, a marble foyer, tree-lined sidewalks, an old brick church, the art museum. It's my Manhattan in Atlanta.

On Saturdays I meet Daddy. We meet for lunch at Cross Roads, famous for seafood. We discuss movies, books, plays. Sometimes a friend or my cousin Ina Sue comes with me to meet Daddy. He asks what we're reading and what films we've seen. He listens to our opinions. He takes us seriously. He treats us like adults. We adore Daddy.

Daddy is trying to shape, or maybe warp, my mind. He wants to pour everything he knows inside me. If the body is an empty vessel for God, my mind is an empty pitcher for Daddy. Daddy knows a lot about a lot of things. A favorite writer is W. C. Brann, a nineteenth-century journalist known as Brann the Iconoclast. A favorite book is Franz Werfel's *The Forty Days of Musa Dagh* about the Armenian genocide. And his least favorite is *Gone with the Wind* that celebrates slavery.

Daddy brings me a copy of *Tropic of Cancer*. He tells me it's a great book. He tells me it was banned like many great books. I understand it was banned because of sex. I know a little about risqué books. Underlined passages from *Peyton Place* and *Lady Chatterly's Lover* circulated around our cabin at camp. After I read the first pages of *Tropic of Cancer*, I shut the book. I shut it in disgust. There's a description of a vagina that makes me squirm. Maybe Daddy wants to shock me. Maybe he wants Henry Miller to loosen me up.

I'm probably wilder than Daddy thinks. I go to large, wild parties at the Dinkler's house where the pool and gardens overflow with teens. Everyone is drinking, dancing, swimming. There's making out and passing out. There's a band by the side of the pool. Hank Ballard and the Midnighters play at these parties. Hank Ballard wrote and sang the original version of "The Twist." Many of his songs are very suggestive. I've listened to his records a hundred times.

My cousin Larry lives with the Dinklers. Mrs. Dinkler hired him to teach her kids to swim. Then he moved into their house. Larry is tall and handsome—and a great swimmer. In high school, he competed in the Havalanta games between Havana and Atlanta. Now he goes to college at UNC.

I'm young when I start dating college boys. Boys who come to Emory and Georgia Tech from other places. Boys who live in Jewish fraternity houses like AEPi and TEP. Boys who have their own cars, play Lenny Bruce records, drink Singapore Slings, and wear Canoe cologne. I spend lots of time at Emory's AEPi house. So much time they elect me to their Sweetheart Court. My boyfriend is an AEPi from North Miami Beach. He's accustomed to integrated places. He takes me to Paschal's La Carrousel, a jazz club where the great jazz artists play. The people who sit closest to the stage are Black. We don't sit near the stage. It feels like an intrusion to sit near the stage. We sit at a table near the bar. By the bar, we can hear the music fine. When the musicians start to play, everyone is quiet. Everyone listens. It's reverential the way we listen. The room is hushed. The music is serious. I pay close attention, but sometimes the music goes beyond me.

The atmosphere, the music, the alcohol, the beautiful Black women and suave Black men make La Carrousel the most sophisticated place I know. I try to look sophisticated, too. I wear a black crepe dress with a low back. I wear pearls and heels and Chanel N°5. I have a fake ID that says I'm twenty-one. In Georgia you have to be twenty-one to drink, but the legal voting age is 18. There's a slogan—*If you're old enough to die for your country, you're old enough to vote.*

When I first visit La Carrousel, the hostess checks my ID. That's not unusual. She has to check my age. Inside my beaded evening bag are my fake ID, my lipstick, my comb. The necessities of night life fit inside a small evening bag.

She asks me, "Are you related to Eddie Brenner?" When I tell her that he's my father, she says, "You're welcome here anytime."

I'm amazed. I had no idea that Daddy went to La Carrousel. When I ask him, he says, "I don't want to talk about it." Mother is in the room. That's why he doesn't want to talk about it. I tell Mother that she should go, too. However, Mother doesn't approve of mingling. She believes in rights but not mingling. She thinks mingling is stepping into other people's business. Or maybe she's afraid. Maybe equality is better in theory than practice.

I never find out about Daddy's secrets. Or his travels across the color line. I think Daddy maybe had another life. I think that would explain why he hardly came home until late at night. Or why my parents fought so much. Or even why they separated. La Carrousel was maybe the place where Daddy felt most comfortable. A place where he could mingle and live the way he wanted.

La Carrousel is one extreme, The Royal Peacock another. It's a music club on Auburn Avenue, the center of Black Atlanta. The great soul musicians play The Peacock. Jackie Wilson is probably the all-time highlight for me.

The entrance to the club is at the top of a tall, narrow staircase—patrons crammed on every step and out the door, hoping to get in. We stand on the stairs until our IDs are checked. When I start going to The Peacock, I'm in tenth grade. We're all underage. We all use fake IDs. Blank drivers' licenses are easily available. All you have to do is type in fake information and pay somebody $1 to laminate it.

Inside the hall are rows of long tables arranged on either side of the stage. There's no dancing, only music. No alcohol, only set-ups. Boys bring liquor in flasks, hidden in paper bags or their pockets. The Peacock and La Carrousel are my first experiences of integration. Unlike Mother, I have no qualms about mingling. I think it's about time.

Before the music, there's often a stripper. She doesn't move much except to take off her clothes. She doesn't shake or dance around. Unlike the fanfare of the Folies Bergère, there's nothing glamorous about it. This is one of the most interesting things I've ever seen. Maybe because she looks indifferent. And bored. I see that it's easy to take off your clothes and not care.

One night a fight breaks out at The Peacock. Seated beside me, a couple starts to fight. Not only shout but push and shove. They roll off their chairs onto the floor. They roll until they're under the table. When I look down, the woman is on top of the man. I think maybe they're humping. I think maybe something sexual is happening. Then I see that she's strangling him. Her hands are around his neck, and she's squeezing as hard as she can. The bouncers flash their lights. They run over to our table. They yank the couple from the floor and throw them out the door.

The Peacock is as far from Buckhead as I ever go. An entirely other reality. It's there that I understand I'll someday find another reality, too.

\*

I return to Camp Sky Lake. I'm no longer a camper. I'm sixteen and a counselor-in-training. I fall in love with Buddy from Miami Beach. Buddy is eighteen with dimples, black curly hair, and a bad attitude. He likes to cuss and break the rules. All the girls have crushes on Buddy. I'm surprised he likes me. After lights-out, we meet at the boathouse. The boathouse is intoxicating—the scent of the pine forest, the scent of the lake, the countless stars and velvet sky. We kiss. We pet. But I'm totally out of my league with Buddy. Buddy wants to go all the way. We fight about my not wanting to go all the way. When we fight, his every other word is a cuss word. It's a lot of work to resist Buddy.

Late hours at the boathouse and long hours with campers wear me down. I'm tired and feverish. My glands are swollen. I'm diagnosed with mononucleosis. Mono is called the "kissing disease," which in my case is accurate. I'm ordered home to recuperate.

Driving back to Atlanta from camp, Daddy tells me he's living with Mother. They aren't separated anymore. They're living together in our apartment. When we get home, they kiss. It's the first time I've ever seen them kiss. It's not a passionate kiss, but it's proof of something. Or so I hope.

After two weeks, I'm allowed to return to camp. Buddy has a new girlfriend. She's also from Atlanta. I know her.

She's an acquaintance. Her parents are friends with my parents. I wonder if they're going all the way. I suspect that's how she stole him away from me. I'm distressed, but I pretend I don't care. I'm relieved I don't have to fight constantly with Buddy. I find another boyfriend. He's from Daytona. A much nicer boy who doesn't cuss or break the rules.

It's my senior year. I go with my parents to hear Dave Brubeck. I go with Daddy to hear Harry Belafonte and Lena Horne at the Atlanta Auditorium. It's a benefit for Dr. King and SCLC. From my seat in the balcony, I can see Dr. King in the wings. He's laughing. Whenever someone on stage makes a joke, he laughs. He's engaged in one of the world's most critical situations, and he laughs. I'm happy he can laugh. Later I learn from my close friend Lynn how much Dr. King loved to laugh and joke around. She was on his staff in Chicago. She called him "Martin." She told me he was a very funny man.

The closed parts of Atlanta are opening. It doesn't affect my school or neighborhood. Buckhead hasn't opened. But it's easy to feel the change. Change is starting to blow around me wherever I go.

Daddy's best friend comes to visit. Daddy went to college with Joe Sugarman. They both went to UNC. All my life I've heard about Joe Sugarman. I've heard Daddy say that Joe Sugarman is a true genius. Joe lives in New York. He works at the New York Public Library. He has had nervous breakdowns. He's an excitable, talkative, animated man. One morning before anyone is up, I hear Joe outside my door. It's six in the morning. Joe is on the telephone in the hall. He tells me he couldn't sleep. He tells me he has been up all night. He didn't have anyone to talk to so he called the long-distance operator. They've been talking for hours. I never knew a person could be so lonely. I think Daddy must be lonely, too.

# 16

# ESCAPE

Mother lets me off at the curb. I have a ticket to Boston and a couple of suitcases. I'm dressed for the occasion in a navy linen dress, navy Pappagallo pumps, pantyhose, and pearls. I'm going away to college. I'm nervous and excited. At Logan I retrieve my suitcases. I find a taxi. I ride from the airport to my dorm. I pay the driver. I add a tip. Things I've never done on my own. Steps that assure me I know what to do.

At the dorm, I meet my roommates—Susan from Danbury, Dodie from Columbus. We're to share a large room. And a new, large life. For a week, we go through orientation. We're squired around Harvard Square and the North Shore. We're taken to buy a green Harvard book bag. We're escorted to Elsie's for roast beef sandwiches with Russian dressing. We're told to expect invitations to mixers with freshman boys.

"A meat market," a sophomore informs us.

By October it's already cold. Colder than February in Atlanta. I don't know how I'll survive the winter. I'm poorly prepared. I think of fur. That's how animals cope. That's how I'll cope, too. The furriers in Copley Square clearly do not trade in used goods. I proceed farther into downtown and the underworld of junk shops and thrift stores. I speculate that where there's charity, I'll find fur. And I'm correct. For ten dollars, I purchase a sheared raccoon coat. An ugly thing that will save me from an ungodly clime.

It's early afternoon on November 22. Rumors have started to fly. In Dallas President Kennedy's motorcade has been attacked. The President has been shot. Most classes are canceled. Most of Boston is on its knees in prayer. My history class isn't canceled. Impatiently, we wait for the professor to finish. Outside our classroom window, we watch the flags drop to half-mast. As soon as the hour strikes, we hurry out. We make our way to the nearest church. Someone hands me a tissue to put on my head. Another hands me a tissue for my tears. At the church, everyone is sobbing.

Six days later is Thanksgiving. Too far to go home, I go to New York. A friend with a sports car drives us. It's a traffic jam all the way. Thanksgiving in New York is a college tradition. Hotels in New York offer special student discounts. The hotel lobbies are mobbed. It's ridiculous how much fun we have in the wake of a national tragedy.

My college education happens mostly outside the classroom. A lecture by Malcolm X, a presentation by James Baldwin, the discovery of Piaf, Nina Simone, and Segovia. An Irish boyfriend and I exchange records—his Beethoven's Fifth for my Beatles. I volunteer at the Kennedy's family apartment on Beacon Hill. We have access to the apartment, a dozen phone lines, and a list of campus contacts at every college in the country. We call to raise funds for the Kennedy Library. It's a nationwide student effort.

Almost weekly, Daddy writes me a single-spaced, one-page letter. Filled with news and political commentary, book and theater reviews, sharp critiques and displays of affection, stories and jokes in a loose, rambling style. The other girls on my floor gather to listen to Daddy's letter. It's a weekly ritual. The letters touch their lives, too.

\*

Undated: *About Tuesday, the remarkable LBJ announced he was coming to Atlanta, and did so, arriving Thursday night, having breakfast with the Georgia legislature, Friday am—on to Gainesville, etc. His reception was fantastic—really wild everywhere—his speech to the legislature emphasized equal rights for everyone and the Crackers cheered even that—this is the first time he has made a strong statement on Civil Rights in the Deep South—this is the first time a President has been in Georgia since FDR—I have decided that this man is a political genius of the FDR stripe—and Linda Bird, who also spoke here, is the greatest 20 year old in history—he may even be better than The Boss, because he has the liberals believing he is conning the conservatives, and vice versa—as a man from the CofC said "He's trying to be elected unanimously"—While I am aware that your generation is dedicated to JFK, you also remember that I was not an aficionado—I respected him intellectually, but doubted his political skills and questioned his warmth—for example, I don't think you can approach a problem like poverty coldly—it requires an emotional dedication, which I think the boy lacked. . . .*

Undated: *This was Operation "Opera Week" in Atlanta and the opera buffs buffed their butts bare with eight Met performances in seven days—We saw only one, Don Giovanni—I think it was magnificent—our seats were somewhere in the left field bleachers, and I didn't have a libretto—the left portion of the stage was out of our range of vision, and I strongly suspect that several murders took place in that sector—I know there were fewer persons on stage at the end than at the beginning. Leontyne Price sang Donna Anna, which while the female lead, was still a smaller part than I would have wished—nevertheless, it was good to be able to hear her—it was my first for this opera too, and I liked it—really sort of frothy with lots of quartets, sextets, etc.—a ghost—maybe it was better without the libretto, because there a moment of shock as electrifying as anything in "Desperate Hours"—This was Price's first appearance in Atlanta—a couple of years ago someone asked Bing when he was going to bring her here and he replied, "When she can leave the airport in a desegregated taxi, drive to a hotel of her choice and eat anywhere she wants". . . .*

Sunday—24 [May 1964]: *This is the way it ends, so this is the way it ends, so this is the way it ends, not with a bang but with a whimper—I think that is Eliot—and he was talking about either the world or life—I ran across it on the frontispiece of "On the Beach"—I'm talking about correspondence since our next communication will be oral—needless to say I've enjoyed immensely talking at you. I think the nicest thing about writing letters is the absence of interruptions. . . . Present schedule is to leave Atlanta, Saturday May 30—spend first night on road, probably somewhere in Virginia—Sunday and Monday nites in Washington with some sightseeing with David the Bomber—into N.Y. probably around noon, Tuesday, June 2—staying N.Y., 2,3,4—driving back a westerly route—to take in Shenandoah and Blue Ridge Parkways—have requested ticket sources to get "Funny Girl", plus any two of "Hamlet", "Dylan", "After the Fall", "The Deputy", "Beyond the Fringe"—we will see what happens—should have four seats for something, all three nights. . . . Find out what you can about the Fair [New York World's Fair]—I would think it would be disastrous to go out there without some sort of plan—I trepidate a little anyway—what I'm really looking forward to is coming back to the hotel and lying down each afternoon—You, of course, as a veteran of Brussels [World's Fair] and Disneyland have much more experience than I—My feet are already throbbing in anticipation. I shall write a report on the event entitled Bunion's Progress—or Long Day's Journey into Plight. . . .*

*

Daddy's father is a butcher at a slaughterhouse in downtown Boston. It's not far from Durgin-Park, an old and famous restaurant. The two link in my mind as Durgin-Park serves jumbo portions of roast beef that hang over the edge of the plate. The visit to the slaughterhouse is only the second time I've met my grandfather. When I was a child, he came to my Aunt Bessie's house in Batesburg, and we met. Otherwise, I've not seen him. The slaughterhouse is not a pleasant place to talk. Even outside on the sidewalk, carcasses on iron hooks are visible through the door.

The next Saturday I take the train to Lowell. Grandpa and his wife Rose pick me up at the station. It's the Sabbath. Rose isn't allowed to cook, but they are allowed to order Chinese food. As we eat, we search for a topic of conversation. School? Movies? Boys? There isn't much to talk about. Rose has a sweet, gentle manner, but my grandfather barely says a word. *My grandfather*, I remind myself, trying to connect. But I fail. As dull and repetitive as it is—awful Chinese food and long silences—I make myself go to Lowell once or twice again. I think it's my duty. Maybe connecting the pieces of my family has always been my duty.

When my roommates go home with me over spring break, Daddy and David meet us at the airport in Beatle wigs. Daddy has discovered a new word—*gear*.

"Everything is gear!" Daddy says.

In the spring, Mother sends up a light wool coat for my birthday. Navy houndstooth with piping on the collar and cuffs. In March there's no sign of spring. In April it snows. However, once the weather begins to warm, I'm transformed from a furry ball to an hourglass in my new coat.

I'm on my way to Cambridge. I'm going to meet a boyfriend. The MTA car is nearly empty. Across the aisle from me are two teenage girls in crinolines and stiletto heels, their hair teased in beehives. I can smell their perfume and hair spray. I'm reading, but as I inspect them, they inspect me—my spring coat, my pumps, my long, straight hair tied with a grosgrain ribbon. They think I'm a snobby college girl. All the signs are there. When the train slows at Central Square, the girls rise to exit. They hold the pole beside me, and as the doors slide back, a fist pounds my shoulder. It's class warfare, and I've been attacked. The enemy has attacked me. They gallop across the platform, giggling with victory. *We won! We won!*

# 17

# GRIEF

Two letters arrive. One letter for me, another for Mother. There is no letter for David. David will be told that Daddy had a heart attack. This is what I'll also say for many years to come. When my children are young, that's what I tell them. "Your grandfather died of a heart attack at forty-nine." I think *heart attack* accurately describes what went wrong with Daddy.

The police find him in an abandoned garage. A few blocks from our apartment house, there's a garage with a bolted door and a car engine running inside. Daddy is in the car. My Uncle Joe comes to tell us that the search for Daddy is over. When he enters our apartment, he doesn't say anything. He shakes his head. I know what the shake means. At such a terrible moment, nothing is real. Everything is surreal. And although I'm not totally surprised, it's a blow. Daddy is dead.

I put the last letter with Daddy's other letters to me. The lively ones from college and camp. As hard as his last letter is to read, it's a treasure. It's a treasure like Daddy himself.

Daddy is buried in the Abelman family plot in the Jewish section of Atlanta's Greenwood Cemetery. Daddy's sister Bessie Brenner Garber and her husband Julius

Garber come with their son Ronnie from Batesburg. Daddy's father Nathan Brenner comes from Boston. Daddy's father is an Orthodox Jew. For a long time, he and Daddy have had little contact. Daddy rejected religion, but the Kaddish is an important Jewish prayer for the dead. Beside the grave, Daddy's father recites the Kaddish. In the July heat, Daddy's father faints.

After Daddy dies, a single red rose comes every day. For twelve days, a rose is delivered in a florist box with an unsigned card and a verse of poetry. I suspect that the roses are from Jimmy Johnson, a wild, freckled country boy who pitches for the University of Georgia. The kind of boy my mother detests. I never find out who sent the roses. After Daddy dies, I don't go out. I give up on Jimmy. I give up on fun. I live in a daze. The first movie I see is *Dr. Zhivago*. Its beautiful theme song will forever remind me of Daddy's death.

I have mixed feelings about his death. Killing yourself is a horrible thing for those left behind. I have mixed feelings about his letter. A treasure, yes, but I'd prefer to think he was too distraught to compose a coherent letter. I'd prefer to think he committed a rash, impulsive, regrettable act. I don't like its deliberate, thoughtful style. Or its assumption about my guilt-free, happy future. Or its reference to the quote by T.S. Eliot.[*] I know the quote. I've read T.S. Elliot and *On the Beach*, a famous book about nuclear destruction. For me the quote has two connotations—the death of one and the death of all.

I don't hold this final act against Daddy. In his letter, he is right. He made his own terrible decision. I'm heartbroken, but I don't blame him. I don't blame anyone. I only wish he had left years ago and saved himself.

* From "The Hollow Men," a poem by T.S. Eliot. *This is the way the world ends/This is the way the world ends/This is the way the world ends/Not with a bang but a whimper.*

## 18

# THE END

*Dearest S—*

I hope that I have the grace to make my last communication brief. When I wrote the business about the bangs and the whimpers, I knew that that was to be my penultimate message. What I am doing is not impulsive. The accelerated debilitation of me, mentally and physically, has forced me to take an action, which I am sure, mercifully you can not understand. I am writing you only because I think that you might confusedly have guilt feelings. I want you to know that you have never committed a sin of omission or commission which in any way affected this terrible decision of mine. You are a wonderful daughter, and as such I think entitled to some sort of explanation. I have long since reached the point at which the pains overwhelmingly outnumber the pleasures—I am also on a downhill skid which can be arrested only by this exorcism. I would not want anyone to see me at the bottom of this hill.

I think of you as a legacy to the world. You are a wonderful child, and I think of your future as "Futures Unlimited." My inability to cope with the world as I found it should not affect you. I have known for 20 years that the world is right and I am wrong—ergo the lack of accommodation is a deficiency in me—your generation is miles ahead of ours. I wish I could stay to see you find and marry the person you love, go *forward with him to the happiness you deserve. I hope you will find forgiveness in your heart for this completely selfish act. I hope you will understand that I have painted myself into a corner and that I must get out. The only thing of which I am really sure is that you are a person of sufficiently mature judgment that you will respect my decision that this is the only way out for me. Forgive me—I do love you.*

*Dad*

\*

Poetry is a great solace. Poetry and music are great solaces. I love to read poetry and write poems. There are many poets I love to read. A. E. Housman's *Shropshire Lad* was the first book of poems I loved. In high school, I wrote poems that my senior English teacher interpreted as a sign of depression. I found her remark strange. I thought loss and disappointment, melancholy and self-reflection were the classic subjects of poetry.

Daddy's favorite poem is "The Garden of Proserpine" by Algernon Charles Swinburne. Whenever I read it, I'm moved by the penultimate stanza.

*From too much love of living,*
*From hope and fear set free,*
*We thank with brief thanksgiving*

*Whatever gods may be
That no life lives for ever;
That dead men rise up never;
That even the weariest river
Winds somewhere safe to sea.*

## 19

# FATHERLAND

When I return to Boston, I don't talk about Daddy. I don't mention his death to any of my friends. When my roommate's sociology class assigns a book called *Suicide*, I don't ask her to remove it from my sight. For weeks I confront this book like punishment and penance. Only once do I break down. I break down after a young man accuses me of never having suffered. His sister was killed in a car accident, and he asserts that I could never understand.

For years I don't believe Daddy is dead. I'm not irrational or crazy. I simply don't believe it. I wonder if this phenomenon affects other people who suddenly lose loved ones. One day you have a father, and the next you don't. It's an adjustment. A physical and mental adjustment. But I don't want to adjust.

When I look up at the sky, I try to picture Daddy's face. His large moon face, the color of cashew with his caterpillar eyebrows and teeth stained by coffee and nicotine. I try to see if he's looking down at me, like Billy Bigelow in *Carousel* looked down from heaven at his daughter and sang, "You'll Never Walk Alone." I try to picture his brown eyes and find them sparkling with humor and pity. His eyes tell me that he wishes he could help. His eyes laugh, but they can't help. Not me, not himself, not anyone. Maybe it was helplessness that killed him.

For years walking or driving, I see parts of Daddy. I see him on sidewalks or leaving restaurants. His back, his neck, his ill-fitting jackets, his cropped hair. I see him in unexpected places far from Georgia. I imagine rushing up behind him and shouting, "Daddy! Daddy!" I want to believe that the body in the car was a mistake. I want to believe he ran away and saved himself.

Daddy was born on November 22, 1914 in Hendersonville, North Carolina, the son of Jewish immigrants from Ukraine. November 22, the same day my oldest grandchild Julian will later be born—my life book-ended by marvelous Daddy and marvelous Julian.

After Kennedy was shot, also on November 22, and Oswald gunned down, Daddy said to me, "That's the end." I thought he meant the end of the world. But maybe he meant himself.

## 20

## FIRENZE

It's my junior year of college when students often go abroad. Mother has decided that we should move to Florence, Italy. Although living in Italy means living with Mother, I'm happy to be leaving the country. We stay in an elegantly appointed *pensione*—spacious rooms, palladium windows, ornate molding, ruched silk drapes, and a view of the river. Mother and I share a room, David sleeps in an alcove. The *pensione* serves two meals. At breakfast the sweet butter is curled in a ribbon, my first hint that Italians pay great attention to details. Italian cars and Italian shoes are famously designed. But grocery bags and matchboxes are beautifully designed, too.

The buildings of Florence are ochre-colored. Almost all the buildings are ochre as well as the river. The monochrome city contrasts with the blue sky. I've never seen such brightness and blueness except in Italian Renaissance paintings. I once thought these paintings were artistic fantasies. But now I know that Florentine artists painted what they saw.

I meet a young Italian. At a street festival, I literally fall into his arms. He is beautiful like everything around him. His baby face and caramel skin, his dark hair and deep dimples, he looks like a giant Cupid. He has a motor scooter. I hop on the back of his scooter, and we cruise around the countryside. He takes me to his family villa in town. From the street, we enter through a massive door in a wall and into a grand courtyard. At the far end of the courtyard is the villa. We wander through a maze of large rooms. Each room is stuffed with couches, tables, chairs, armoires, lamps, chandeliers, mirrors, mantles. Each piece with a price tag. His father is an antique dealer. They live in a giant antique store.

After a month, we move to a rooftop apartment a few yards from the Arno. From our balcony, we can see the topsy-turvy dwellings by the river, the Ponte Vecchio, and the top of Brunelleschi's dome. The gold ball and the cross on top of the Duomo mark the center of town. And maybe the center of western civilization.

David attends the American School. Mother goes to art school. I go to the Uffizi for an hour every day. I also start classes at the language school for *stranieri*. My new friends are *stranieri* like me. Either European, Middle Eastern, or American. After class we sit in coffee bars. At night we go out dancing. Sometimes a young American millionaire invites us to eat at Sabatini's. He drives a Ferrari, and behind his back, we call him "Goldfinger." An Italian teenager invites us to her birthday party. In a narrow room lined with chairs, Italian girls and boys sit opposite each other. Chaperones sit beside them. The girls wait for the boys to cross the empty room and ask them to dance. I understand. I grew up in a highly mannered atmosphere. I too used to obey the rules of decorum. But I've broken away. I live with my mother, but I'm independent. I walk around at any hour. I live my own life.

Over the fall and winter, we take excursions. We go to a beach near Pisa. We go to Venice. At Christmas we travel to Pompeii and Capri, empty of tourists. Without cars, Capri feels like a toy village.

Mother makes friends with Pat, a divorcee from Connecticut. Pat has come to Italy to find a husband. Mother is relatively young and beautiful, but she has no interest in a husband. She says that Daddy spoiled her for any other man. She says she'll never meet another man as brilliant as Daddy. She speaks about Daddy with reverence and awe. When he was alive, she couldn't stand him. When he committed suicide, she resented him. Now she idolizes him.

James Baldwin stops in Florence en route from Turkey to France. He plans to speak at a local bookstore. I've already read most of his books. I heard him speak at Harvard. Mother and I attend the reading together. She has read his books, too. I sit as close as possible, enraptured by his voice and outrage.

The next day on the Ponte Vecchio, I see him. I muster my courage. I approach Mr. Baldwin. "Can you come to tea?" I blurt. And point to our apartment at the far end of the bridge.

Mr. Baldwin shakes his head. He doesn't have time. Maybe he senses how hard it was for me to speak to him. Or maybe my earnestness touches him. Whatever the reason, he says, "Bless you, my child."

My boyfriend is French. He's handsome and tall with a battered Belmondo face. *Joli laid.* He's a photographer with artistic ambitions. I'm twenty, he's thirty. He pressures me to have sex. If I want to be with him, sex is part of it. Since Buddy I've resisted going all the way. I've had boyfriends, but I haven't gone all the way. Now it's a burden—and an embarrassment.

Michel and I make love in his cheap hotel room. He puts a towel underneath me, expecting I will bleed. But there's no blood. He thinks I only pretended to be a virgin. When I get home, it's no later than usual. Mother never waits up for me, but when I open the door, she's in the middle of the room. She's furious. She yells and throws a glass. The glass explodes against the wall. It's as if she knows I had sex. In the morning, the landlady asks us to move out. The neighbors have complained. She says she can't have these kinds of disturbances in the building. Mother is mortified. She promises there will be no more disturbances.

Michel earns his living by hustling tourists at beaches in Spain and the Canary Islands. It's a drifter's life, meeting women and renting beach equipment. He's in Florence to learn Italian. He already speaks English, Dutch, German, Spanish, and of course, French. He and

I go on trips. We go to Fasching in Munich. We go to Rome. I don't have money. I have to beg money off my mother. Or let Michel pay. I don't like either arrangement.

To make money, I start to model. My first job is for a makeup company where they show my face with and without lipstick, rouge, eyeliner, eyeshadow, and mascara. In another shot, they throw water on me. I pretend that I've just come out of the sea, and my makeup hasn't streaked. The company's owner takes me to his factory. As part of my payment, he asks me to pick out whatever I want. He tries to kiss me, but as soon as I resist, he gives up.

Word-of-mouth spreads about TV ads. My blond German friend tells me they want foreigners. I look Italian, but they invite me to come along. Six of us are driven to the countryside where we romp up and down a hillside and ride bikes around a castle. The ad is for luncheon meat. Our picnic is supposed to be the highlight of a fun day. But I can barely bite into the sandwich. The mortadella makes me gag.

In spring Michel leaves Florence. I've saved enough money so I can travel and meet him. Mother tries to stop me. She thinks I'm going to marry Michel. Because he's charming and older, she thinks I'll marry him.

Mother doesn't give me much credit. I don't give her reason to give me much credit. But I have no intention of marrying Michel. I'm too young to marry. Too young and too inexperienced. Also, he's conceited. I haven't yet learned that conceited people are mostly insecure. And he's not well-educated. I haven't yet understood how the French education system disadvantages the working class. Nonetheless, I'm attached to him. Because he's my first lover, I'm very attached. He has a certain control over me. It was this foreseeable control that kept me from having sex all these years.

I take a train to meet Michel in Perpignan, his hometown. We stay in an empty apartment that his parents own. After a few days, we travel to Barcelona by car and to Mallorca by ferry. In Palma we see El Cordobés, the rock star of bullfighting. I have a mysterious affinity for flamenco music and dance and the Roma people. Even the brutality of the bullfight fascinates me. It's as if I lived another life in another place.

On the far side of the island from Palma, Michel and I stay in a small, primitive stone house in a village. At a nearby beach, he works at a concession stand that rents umbrellas, lounge chairs, inner tubes and floats. I write and read and hang around. I admire how Michel manages to live like he wants with almost no effort.

I've promised Mother to return. I leave Michel in Spain. I take a train back to Florence. A long, complicated trip, with seven train changes and layovers. Soon David and I will take a ship from Italy to New York. Soon Mother will fly home from London.

Mother thinks I'll never meet a decent man. Or make a decent marriage. She thinks I'm lost. And undoubtedly, she blames Daddy.

# 21

# EUROPEAN REPRISE

In early June, David and I sail from Genoa. It's a full-sized ocean liner repurposed for students. Most passengers are Europeans en route to the States. The Americans are a tiny group, all of us depressed. During our ten days at sea, we sit on the deck, smoking and complaining and recounting our adventures. We are sorry to be going home. On the deck are exuberant Swiss and German youth. They're doing calisthenics and throwing themselves into the icy pool. They are readying themselves for America. We want to tell them, *Go back! Europe is better! Go back!* But none of us speak the same language. They speak arrival. We speak return.

On the ship, David is my shadow. He follows me from the cabin to the deck, the deck to the cabin. We sleep and eat together, three extravagant meals a day. Dinner consists of several courses served with wine and cheese and pastry trays for dessert. Halfway through the trip the fish is stinky, the cheese is hard, the tablecloths and napkins soiled. Meals deteriorate like our moods. Nights are worse than days, with silly entertainments.

We're relieved to get off the ship. We're relieved to get to Atlanta. I desperately need to learn a practical skill. With a practical, portable skill, I can go anywhere and work. I enroll in secretarial school for typing and shorthand. Every day we practice typing to Herb Alpert & the Tijuana Brass. I hate that music. I hate shorthand. I never want to be a secretary.

At Daddy's grave, I vowed to do what Daddy never did. It was almost unconscious, the vow. I told myself that I would learn when it was time to leave. Now I tell myself it's time to leave. It's a simple, frightening decision. If truth be told, it's not a decision. It's instinct.

In the end, I wrestle a bit of cash. As the child of a deceased vet, I'm entitled to a stipend to study. As long as I'm in school, the government will send me a stipend every month. I register for Daddy's veterans pension. I fly from New York to Paris with a bag of clothes and *The Complete Works of Shakespeare*. I carry the names of three cheap hotels. At Les Invalides, I call each one. In bad French, I ask for a room. It doesn't go well. Neither my French nor a room. *Complet*, the hoteliers say, and hang up.

I'm exhausted from the long trip. I'm confused. I pace around the great hall of Les Invalides, mumbling. *What do I do now? What do I do now?* I call the Alliance française to see if they have a suggestion. They say they can help. They say they help all their students find lodging. The one caveat is that I have to enroll in the school.

I store my bag in a locker. I catch the Metro to Montparnesse. I proceed with the entrance exam, the photo, the ID card. I'm officially enrolled. But now the housing office is closed. A couple of French boys are hanging around. They're here to meet foreign girls. They notice my distress. They ask if they can help. They drive me to Les Invalides. They find me a room for the night. They check on me the next day. I resist my mother's curse. I'm lucky to have met them.

I fill out the papers to enroll at the Sorbonne, but I'm in Paris to become a poet. It's baffling to know how to become a poet. With a notebook and pen, I walk around trying to become a poet. I have faith that Paris will make me a poet. Artists have always come to Paris. They've come from every continent for inspiration. Henry Miller came to Paris. I now read Henry Miller. I now love his books.

I believe I'm following in the footsteps of all the other poets. But in fact, I'm bumbling around. And I'm lonely. I tell myself not *lonely*, only alone. I convince myself that loneliness is unimportant. Only practice and persistence are important. I follow my own naive guide to making my own life.

American Express is where I get my mail. Every few days, I take the Metro to *Opéra* to check my mail. Michel writes to me. He's coming to Paris from the Canary Islands. He wants to see me. I surprise myself because I don't want to see him. I want to hold onto my life in Paris. *My Paris*. I know if I see him, he'll reclaim me. He'll take over. He'll dictate where we go and what we do.

I write back and ask him to let me know when he arrives. And where he's staying. I'll contact you, I say.

Then a bizarre thing happens. On Michel's first night in Paris, he's walking up Boulevard Saint-Michel. At the same time, I'm walking down. At night when I walk, I look at the sidewalk. To avoid eye contact, my eyes are cast down. Eye contact can get you in trouble. With lonely young men, it can especially get you in trouble. They might mistake a glance for an invitation. That's how Michel sees me before I see him. He blocks me so we nearly collide. I look up. It's Michel!

We go back to my room. I've moved out of my hotel on Rue Jacob. I now live in a *chambre de bonne* near the Jardin du Luxembourg. I'm happy to see him, but I'm also reserved. He can see I've changed. He can see I'm not trying to please him. I'm no longer susceptible to his charms. I'm no longer in his orbit.

"You've changed," he says. "I like you better."

But my gain is his loss. I no longer need him. Or want him. Or love him.

Ten months in Italy and now in France, I'm persuaded that I can fix my own course. I declare who I am—Poet, Rebel, Lover!

## 22

# ALLEGRO MA NON TROPPO

There's no way to remember everything. There's no reason to remember everything. There's no reason to tell all the stories. For this half of the book, I only want to tell a few more. Some aren't so interesting, but I tell them so that you, dear reader, will better understand.

In Paris I meet a wonderful bohemian family. I first meet Jean Pie. We meet on the movie set of *Woman Times Seven*, a comedy starring Shirley MacLaine and directed by Vittorio De Sica. Jean Pie and I are extras in the film. I answered an ad. Jean Pie got the job because his brother is working on the film. Jean Pie and I fall in love so fast that he moves into my *chambre de bonne* almost the next day.

Then I meet his parents and siblings. Their lives revolve around art, politics, films, and books. He and I begin to hop from place to place. If his mother is on vacation, we stay in her large apartment. After I break my leg, we move to his grandmother's apartment in Neuilly with an elevator and a library of English books. We spend long weekends in Busseau with his father Henri and his stepmother Hérisson. We live in the hayloft of their barn. They treat us tenderly, like newborn lovers. Hérisson brings us breakfast in bed. Henri and Hérisson are both translators. They translate English and American fiction into French. They've translated Capote, John le Carré, Dahl, Doctorow, Hammett, Chester Himes, Philip Roth, Philip K. Dick, none of whom I've yet read. In their lives, I see a blueprint for mine.

After a year, I leave France. When Jean Pie reports for compulsory military service, I return to Atlanta. There, I plan to get a college degree and go back to Paris. I live in my mother's apartment. I sleep in my brother's room. David is away in Florida at a school for difficult teenagers. He isn't difficult but different. Being different makes the situation difficult. There are few places for him to go.

Mother and I live separate lives. Sometimes she blows up. Sometimes I break down. I'm a working adult and living at home. I work as a proofreader at a pornography publishing company. I go to a state college and join SDS, a small group of anti-war students. I have a new boyfriend. Paige and I move into a house near Piedmont Park with another couple, Steve and Nicole. The four of us create an outpost of Newsreel—the film company that produces films about the Black Panthers, the New York garbage strike, the Columbia student strike, et al.

Nicole and I show Newsreel films at colleges, high schools, and churches. At a Black high school, we show the film about the Panthers. After the film, all the students want to join the revolution. Their response is unusual. Usually, our audiences are combative. Nicole is French but accused of being Cuban. We're both accused of peddling communist propaganda. In the beginning, it's hard for me to argue with strangers. But I learn. I rebut their accusations. I challenge them with accusations of my own. I learn to defend myself and the politics in the films.

I no longer live in Buckhead. I live in a different Atlanta. Atlanta has become a magnet for young freaks from all over the South. With illusions and disillusions, they descend on Atlanta's Fourteenth Street. There are head shops that sell water pipes and restaurants that cater to macrobiotic diets. The Allman Brothers play free concerts in Piedmont Park. *The Great Speckled Bird* is the local underground paper that publishes radical news.

I've crossed the line into another world—not over the ocean but down the street.

# 23

# GO WEST!

Paige receives a fellowship for graduate school. He'll study for an MFA in photography with Van Deren Coke at the University of New Mexico in Albuquerque. We pack our VW van with our belongings and our dog. We move to Albuquerque. The adobe buildings, the dusty landscape, the barren mountains, the dry air, it's an alien place. We're accustomed to lush green land filled with rivers and lakes. It takes months to acclimate. It takes months to recognize the desert's beauty. But once we do, we embrace the desert. We embrace the brown river and earth, the spectacular sunsets, the dramatic monsoons, the mountains and mesas.

Mother and David visit us in New Mexico. These will be my last moments with David. My last *real* moments for the next thirty years.

\*

When we lived in Albuquerque, David sent a letter to Paige.

*Dear Paige, I have something to tell you, and it is very important. My mother has been picking on me everyday and*

*I can't take any more, and she said to me that she doesn't love me any more, and doesn't care for me any more. I want to live my own life, but she won't let me. There are only two things for me to do, either join the service or get a job, and my own place to live. She even made me go to a college I didn't want to go to.*

*Love, David*

\*

Everything feels momentous. The present and future feel momentous. It's the Vietnam War. We protested in Atlanta. We protest in Albuquerque. In the wake of the murders at Kent State, a large campus protest is scheduled. Paige and cohorts plan to document it with photos and film. Unexpectedly, the National Guard arrives on campus. They arrive in gas masks and riot gear. They arrive armed with teargas, guns, and bayonets. They march shoulder-to-shoulder in military formation across the plaza. Then suddenly, they lower their bayonets and charge.

On May 8, 1970, eleven students are bayoneted by the New Mexico National Guard. Stabbed in the hip, arm, and thigh, their wounds require medical attention. For months their blood is preserved on the university plaza with polyurethane.

The excitement, the upheavals, the growing pains, the music, the drugs, the poetry, the recklessness, the sex, the magic, the insanity, it's hard to describe without cliches. I join *Best Friends*, a poetry collective for women. I learn to cook and sew. I go to readings. I pursue esoteric interests. We visit Jemez Hot Springs in the snow. We attend Christmas Eve mass and Native American dances at the pueblos on the Rio Grande. On the twenty-fifth anniversary of the atomic bombs dropped on Japan, we plant a tree at the Los Alamos

National Laboratory. Paige makes jewelry with beads and shells. I make puppets and embroider "paintings" on felt. Paige teaches at the university. I work at the university press. There is usually a posse of young men at the house, smoking pot and drinking beer with Paige. He and I bicker over household chores. We bicker over feminism and the division of labor. The times are full. Our lives are full. But Paige and I don't survive. We hurt each other. We separate.

I move to Corrales, a village by the river. I fall in love with a poet. We leave our homes with no place to go. We crash around. We sleep on floors. We ignore everything but each other. We make plans to go away. We leave New Mexico and travel to New York. We take a drive-away from Manhattan to Miami. From Miami we fly to Cozumel. We have little money. We plan to travel until our money runs out. On Isla Mujeres we stay in a hammock hotel. For a few cents a night, we string our hammocks between palm trees. We travel around the Yucatán. We visit ancient ruins. We hitchhike to Chiapas and cross the border into Guatemala. We ride on rickety buses and third-class trains. For months we travel around.

After I find out I'm pregnant, we head home. First to Oaxaca and then a week in Mexico City. From Mazatlán we take a train to the border. The train decouples in the middle of the night, with Stephen's half going to Nogales and my half to Tijuana. Alone, broke, and pregnant, I have to make decisions. I have to be resourceful. I have to grow up.

For a few days, I stay with Dede. Dede is a great friend. She lives near Los Angeles in Sierra Madre Canyon. For a few days, I recuperate with her. I've decided to move to San Francisco. In San Francisco I have my friend Melanie from Atlanta. In Oakland I have my friends Scott and Claudia, whom I met in the Yucatán. San Francisco is where I'll start a new life with my baby.

Dede and I drive up Interstate 5. I stay in San Francisco. I sign up for welfare. I find a doctor. Then I contact my friends in Oakland. They live in a cottage on Raymond Street. With their help, I rent an airy flat around the corner from them. I'm pregnant. Claudia is pregnant. Our neighbor Amelie is pregnant. Scott builds us a communal laundry. Scott drives us around. Scott cooks and comforts. Scott is my proxy husband.

Amelie and I have a past connection. I'd heard stories of a young woman named Amelie from my friend Rosemary in Atlanta. She talked about Amelie because her brother Addison and Amelie got married. After they met at the Newport Folk Festival, they ran off to Mexico to marry.

In Buckhead Addison stood out. His long hair, his earring, his poncho made him stand out. In high school Rosemary and I looked up to him. But then he and Amelie moved away. Rosemary and I moved away, too. When I visited her in Brooklyn, I asked about Addison and Amelie. Her brother lived in Nepal. She didn't know what happened to Amelie. Less than a year later, Amelie and I are neighbors and friends.

I find furniture at the flea market and baby clothes at the thrift store. I find useful and useless things in "free" boxes around Berkeley. I stay busy. Busy is how I ward off my fear. I tell myself that having a baby is a natural, normal thing to do. But being alone and having a baby is not so normal. I'm fortunate to have Amelie and Claudia and Scott. We're fortunate to have each other. That I'm unmarried doesn't matter. I'm not living in Buckhead. I'm not living in conventional society. I'm not interested in a conventional life. I'm not interested in a job. I'm interested in being a mother and writing poems. Although I have a college degree and a few practical skills, my outlook is impractical. I'm a single mother-to-be living on welfare.

I also understand that I'm rationalizing. I grew up with privileges. I grew up with certain conventions. It's hard to totally dump them. I wish Stephen were here. I wish he cared enough to be here. I wish things weren't so complicated. I wish I didn't have to totally take care of myself. Daddy encouraged me to believe that I could do whatever I wanted. Daddy was a feminist. Mother was fiercely independent. I learned from both of them.

Now I'm improvising. I'm not sure what to do. I'm afraid. But I think I can make it be okay.

# 24

# THE END OF THE BEGINNING

"Something is wrong with your brother." It's Mother. I can barely hear her. Her voice is shaky. She's hard to understand. "You have to come here and help."

Mother says *your brother*, not David. Like she used to say *your father*, not Eddie. *Your grandmother, your aunt.* It's the way she disconnects from the family. Nonetheless, there's no doubt that David is having a crisis. He has locked himself in his apartment and won't come out. The landlady can't get him to open the door. Mother can't get him to open the door. Day and night, he cries out. But he refuses to open the door. He's disturbing the other tenants. The landlady says she has to evict him. She says if he doesn't leave, she'll call the police.

The next day, I fly to Atlanta. From the airport, Mother drives me to Decatur. Decatur is where David lives. He lives in an apartment near the junior college where he takes classes.

"I'm the only one who believed David would go to college," Mother says.

It's true. No one believed except her. She believed so much that she pressured David. He could have had a simple job. He liked tinkering. He could have repaired bikes and lived modestly. Mother wanted to prove something. She was determined to prove that David was smart by her standards—hers and society's. It's hard to know if her belief was more about him or herself. Her friends' children graduated from prestigious schools. With professional, prestigious careers. David and I are disappointments. There's little she can say about us. There's nothing she can brag about. Poetry doesn't count. My publishing a book doesn't count. Although she's a serious painter, she knows that art is rarely valued. And poetry valued least of all.

Located near David's apartment is a diner. Once a day, the diner is where David goes to eat. Mother tells me David is probably inside. My assignment is go into the diner and persuade David to go with me to a doctor.

David is seated alone in a booth. I walk in and wave at him, as if he's expecting me. I tell the waitress that I'm his sister. I tell her that I've come from California. David is happy to see me. He hops up, and we hug.

"Do you mind if I sit down?" I ask.

I sit across from him. I order something to drink. I make small talk. Then I suggest we go to a doctor to get him help.

"I don't need help," he says.

He doesn't want to hear that he needs help. He doesn't want to see a doctor. He only wants to enjoy his turkey sandwich and go back to his apartment.

The next day, I go back to the diner. David is there at the same time. He's eating the same food as the day before—a turkey sandwich, potato salad, pickles, coleslaw, a slice of cake, and a large Coke. I think this must be the only meal David eats.

He's no longer happy to see me. He's now suspicious of me.

"You need help," I say gently. "I'll go with you to the doctor. We can go together."

David gets increasingly agitated.

He asks, "Do you have a gun? Do you plan to shoot me?"

I assure him that I have no gun. I say that I would never hurt him. I tell him that I'm here to help. I beg him to trust me. I beg him to listen. But I fail to convince him.

David jumps up and runs out of the diner.

No one knows what to do. No one is sure what's wrong, but something awful has happened to David. He's having some kind of breakdown. He thinks I have a gun. He thinks, of all the people in the world, I want to shoot him.

Mother must make a decision. A terrible decision. Since David won't leave his apartment, he must be removed. To avoid eviction and perhaps arrest, he must be forcibly removed. The door must be forced open and David taken out.

Mother asks Duncan to help. Duncan is my cousin Nancy's husband. I don't know what Duncan does. I'm not with him inside the apartment. I'm outside the apartment house with Mother. But David is dragged out of his apartment. We stand in the street, while he's dragged into an ambulance.

The doors of the ambulance close, and we watch it roll away. When I think of this moment, this terrible moment, I see the horizon. The street, the ambulance, the horizon. I see the ambulance moving towards the horizon into a terrible unknown. I hear the echo of David's voice. He's shouting. I can't remember if he really shouted. Or if I heard the shouts exploding inside him. His shouts surround my memory of the ambulance as it moves towards the horizon and disappears. David, the shouts, the ambulance, they all disappear.

Anna Aarons and Morris Abelman (circa 1915)

Evelyn and Rita Abelman (circa 1927)

Essie, Edward, Rebecca, Nathan Brenner (Bar Mitzvah circa 1927)

Edward Brenner (circa 1938)

BESSIE BRENNER (CIRCA 1940)

Rita Abelman Brenner (circa 1940 by Leonid Skvirsky)

Rita Abelman Brenner (circa 1976 by Bill Fibben)

Morris Abelman

ANNA AARONS ABELMAN

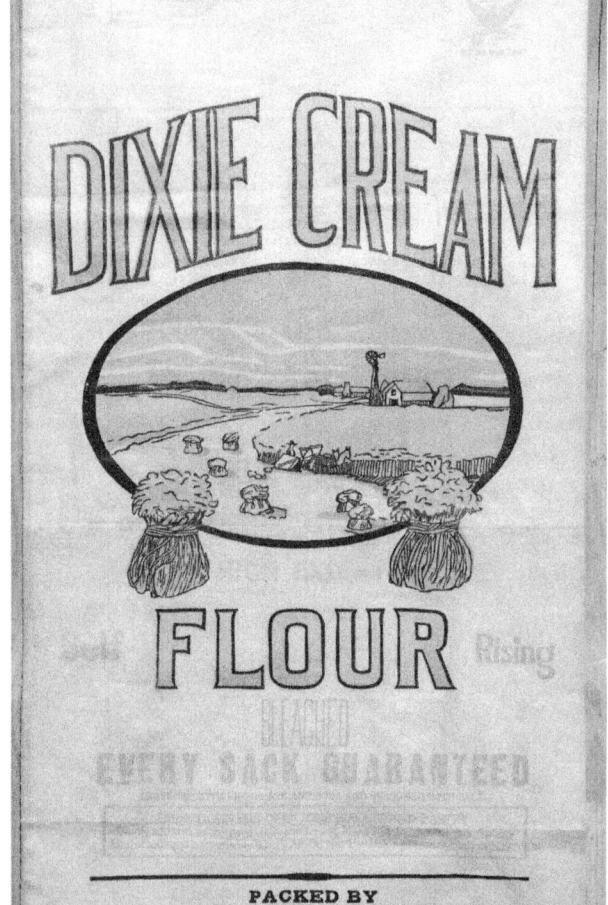

Puritan Mills flour sack

Puritan Mills, Atlanta, Georgia (no longer in business)

# PART 2

# THE END

*Every particle of dust on a patch of earth
Was a sun-cheek or brow of the morning star;
Shake the dust off your sleeve carefully—
That too was a delicate, fair face.*

—The Ruba'iyat of Omar Khayyam

David and Summer Brenner (circa 1998)

## 25

## EMERALD ISLE

When the wing of the plane tilts, everything tilts. The fuselage tilts, the tail and opposite wing tilt, the pilot and co-pilot, the cabin and passenger seats, the passengers buckled in their seats, the stewards and stewardesses buckled in their seats, the sinks and toilets in the lavatory, the movie screen and figures in the movie tilt. Through the clouds we tilt, banking to the east. Then, just as we've accustomed ourselves to tilting and reasoned that the plane is not crashing sideways into the earth, we straighten up. We are no longer tilting. We have sliced through the clouds. They are now above us. We are in view of the city, the verdant plots and parks beneath us. It is green in all directions. All of it is green except for the gray arteries of roads, the buildings, and the swaths of Georgia red clay. We are close enough to see cars, streams of them. We are close enough to see the color of cars, but it is the vivid green we notice. Atlanta is dazzlingly green.

I hold my breath while the plane lands. It's a superstition to hold one's breath when you pass through a tunnel or over a bridge or by a cemetery. It's superstition and custom. Mostly, I hold my breath for the task close at hand. Once I'm in Atlanta, it is very close at hand. Close and unavoidable.

I hold my breath and plug my ears, so I don't have to hear the roar of the brakes when the plane lands. We bounce down the runway. I stop holding my breath. I unplug my ears. Around me, everyone looks relieved. We have landed safely. We are coasting to our gate. We can't yet rise because the plane is still in motion, but we are on the ground. Despite the task at hand, it's ever so much better to be on the ground. The plane finally stops. We gather our belongings. We nod to the pilot who stands by the cockpit. We mutter our thanks to the stewards and stewardesses. Everyone says, "Thank you." We are the epitome of politeness. We are now in the South.

We pass from the element of air to the element of earth. We pass the threshold from the plane to the airport. From the gate, I walk towards the main terminal. Most people do not walk. Most people take the tram. Most people can't imagine walking. The Atlanta airport is huge. It's often cited as the busiest airport in the world. After a long plane ride, I'm glad to make the long walk. The wide carpeted walkway is a straight, empty path. Along the way I pass wall art and sculptures. They are there to be looked at in case someone decides to walk, which hardly anyone does.

When I reach the main terminal, I bypass the baggage claim. I do not need to claim baggage. I roll my suitcase behind me. I roll it directly to MARTA. MARTA is the mass transit network in Atlanta. MARTA is outside the air-conditioned terminal. Its platform is up a flight of stairs. On the platform, I stand and wait for the train. Waiting for MARTA, I inhale the air. The nature of the air is the nature of my entire childhood. A childhood riddled with contradictions like the air itself—sweet, portentous, cruel, yielding, noisy, deadly, and alive.

A train soon comes to carry me north and west. I'm heading to Buckhead. The name alone is mysterious. BUCK HEAD. I know it inch-by-inch, learned like multiplication tables, fixed and familiar, squares in relationship to other squares. Despite the bustle of the new, updated Buckhead, it's all familiar.

Buckhead was once filled with trees, vines, brush, rocks, and animals. The land intersected with creeks and springs. Named by the Native people who lived here—and forgotten. The people of the Cherokee and the Muscogee Creek tribes. By the time I make its acquaintance, buildings and roads cover the ground. Commerce fills the corners. Filling stations, beauty parlors, diners, a pharmacy, a movie theater, the library, and postoffice.

Around Buckhead's center are miles of lofty homes, mansions and houses that look like villas and châteaus, all of them familiar. Not the particulars. The particulars are of no importance. The particulars come and go. The Texaco station comes and goes—replaced by a café with a misspelled French name. But the psychic topography does not change. The subtleties of vacancy and fullness, void and grace, do not change. They remain layered with familiarity.

MARTA and I zip through Buckhead, moving farther north and east to Dunwoody. Dunwoody was a rural village when I was growing up. It's a suburb now. My young cousin Kimberly lives in a condo in Dunwoody in a complex with a hundred condos, surrounded by complex after complex of condos.

Kim and her mother Nancy pick me up at the MARTA station. Nancy is my first cousin. She grew up in Atlanta, too. We grew up together. She now lives in the mountains but has driven two hours to MARTA to pick me up. We plan to stay with Kim. We plan to eat in restaurants in the mall and sleep in Kim's condo. We plan to laugh our heads off.

# 26

# MOTHER

For years Mother has complained about her stomach. Whenever I talk to her, she complains. We used to talk every Sunday. I used to dread our Sunday call. Sunday mornings were ruined because of what I anticipated. I anticipated setting her off. Something in our conversation was bound to set off her ferocious temper. Neutral conversation was impossible. Reasonable conversation went out of control. If I tried to be open, that's what happened. Instead of talking, I listened. I listened to Mother say whatever she was thinking. Anything that came to mind.

Years ago a psychiatrist advised my mother to repress her impulse to say whatever came to mind. *Whoever heard of a psychiatrist telling someone to repress?* Mother asked me. She found it hilarious.

It was only hilarious because she had no idea what her mouth inflicted on others. She considered her responses acts of honesty. Repressing would be dishonest. Although her responses were often mean, they were also sometimes correct. Painfully and bitterly correct. From her I learned that honesty and truthfulness are not the same. I learned that kindness is sometimes more important than honesty.

During our years of Sunday conversations, she'd berate me about marriage. And finding a suitable husband. *While you still have your looks*, she said repeatedly. *While you still have your looks*. Meaning, while my looks could wield some power. The power of both huntress and bait.

If my listening went on too long, so long that she thought I wasn't paying attention, I'd mention an innocuous thing. I should have learned. There was no such thing as *innocuous*. There was a penal code, ever-changing. There were rules I didn't know. Weapons I never mastered. It was impossible to anticipate what would trigger an explosive reaction. Or the subsequent crime and punishment. But both were inevitable.

I'd mention the children. Or a dinner party with friends. A dinner party particularly enraged her.

*Why do you entertain? Why do you bother?*

The crime. *You do things for your friends but not for me.*

The penalty. *I'm not sending you money so you can feed your friends.*

*Oh? You* went *to a dinner party? That's better. They're reciprocating.*

*You asked me to send money for your birthday. I'm not sending money for dinner parties. That gives me no pleasure. Go to Saks like other women. Spend $50 and charge it to me. That gives me pleasure. I'm not sending money to feed your friends.*

*I'm so mad at you. You said something ugly about your*

*brother. The last time you saw him, you said he looked depressed. Don't you know how brilliant he is? Don't you know he could have run your grandfather's company? And made us millions if something hadn't made him sick?*

For her ailments, Mother has gone to many doctors without success. They can't figure out what's wrong. Year after year, their tests show nothing. Apparently, she's in pain without cause. She's uncomfortable for no reason. She complains to doctors who refuse to call her back. She yells at their receptionists. She finds no sympathy from their nurses. And no cure from their medicines. Her doctors are stupid and incompetent. Her lawyers and brokers are stupid and incompetent. Her brokers try to cheat her. Her lawyers can't be trusted. She hates them all. She hates Atlanta. She hates the stupid, incompetent people who claim to be professionals.

Several times Mother has asked me, *Get me a poison pill.*

She asks me to ask a doctor for a poison pill. She wants me to mail it to her. Over and over, she says, *I'm ready to die.* She says, *I've had a marvelous life.* Sometimes she asks, *Haven't I had a marvelous life?*

She traveled everywhere. She went everywhere. *Where haven't I been?* she asks. Then she remembers India. *OK, I missed India.* But almost everywhere else.

*We lived in Florence, remember? Do you remember when we lived in Florence? I came to visit you in Paris. You had a broken leg. Do you remember?* She took the *Queen Mary* over. She calls it, *The Queen.*

*I've had a marvelous life*, she says. *I painted wonderful paintings. Don't you agree?*

Yes, I agree. She painted wonderful paintings. While she received some recognition, it wasn't enough.

*I should have sold my paintings for small fortunes. But life has been really marvelous.*

Mother liked to buy designer clothes. She shopped for clothes at Rich's, J.P. Allen, Frohsin's—wherever French, Italian, and American designers were sold. But when Atlanta became a boomtown, designers opened individual boutiques at Lenox Square and Phipps Plaza. Mother started to peddle her paintings to the boutiques. Managers found them interesting. A painting by Mother could lend an arty ambience to the store. In exchange for paintings, they let her pick out clothes. Mother bartered her art for clothes.

*Don't you remember how resourceful I was? Don't you remember how beautiful my clothes were?*

My friends in California, they remember. They'd admire her shoes, her hat, her jacket, her purse.

*This old Gee-van-chee?* she'd sneer. Trying to give the tricky syllables of *Gi-ven-chy* a French accent.

*I'm going to die poorer than I was born. That's my biggest regret*, she says.

When Coca-Cola was starting, her father was asked to invest. He decided against it. He decided soda pop was too risky. It's the only thing Mother ever held against her father. If he'd invested in Coca-Cola, she'd still be rich. Very rich.

Mother doesn't want to die in her apartment. She doesn't want her neighbors to see her dead. Every morning she puts on lipstick. If she dies in her apartment, she wants to be sure she's wearing lipstick.

I've inquired about places for her to live. She doesn't want to go to an old-age home. She's adamant. She doesn't want to be in a strange place with strangers.

*I wouldn't be happy anywhere so it's pointless to move.*

She wants to be in her own place, but she doesn't want anyone to see her. She wants to fade away. She says, *I want to crawl into the woods and let an animal eat me.*

I don't push her. I know these places are horrible. Grandma was in an old-age home. It was horrible. When I visited the father of a friend at an old-age home in Oakland, a woman accosted me in the hall. She asked me, *What am I supposed to do now?* She asked everyone she met, *What am I supposed to do now?*

Her question startled me. It struck me as the root question of existence. And now away from everything familiar, she had no idea what to do.

I'm used to Mother's complaints—and repetitions. Repetition is expected when people get older. But her recent helplessness surprises me. I'm not used to her helplessness. She's nearly incoherent. She has nearly stopped driving. She has stopped going to the grocery store. She only drives around the corner to Chick-fil-A to get a chicken sandwich. She craves chicken sandwiches and chocolate. She can eat a whole chocolate cake at one sitting.

She doesn't read anymore. She used to be a great reader. She read Simone de Beauvoir and Kathy Acker. She was savvy and urbane. She doesn't paint anymore. She used to go to museums and galleries. She read art magazines and followed news of her favorite painters, Philip Guston and de Kooning. But she has no interest in painting.

Now she rants against George W. Bush. She rants against hippies and feminists. She was appalled when she thought I might be a hippie or a feminist. Appalled when I had a home birth and nursed my baby in public. Worst of all were my armpits. She thinks armpit hair is a disgrace.

Mother only loves to watch old movies with her favorite old movie stars. She loves Norma Shearer and Myrna Loy. She watches them on TV. If the movies are new, she complains about the young actresses.

*They aren't beautiful. They aren't stars. There's nothing to see when Julia Roberts is on the screen.*

In the past, Mother would make pronouncements. *I need to get away*, she'd say. Because of her stomachaches, she thought if she got away she'd feel better. Getting away would calm her nerves.

*But where can I go? Where are the nice people?* By *nice* she means women with expensive purses.

*Should I go to a spa in Arizona? Or on a cruise?* Then she remembers that people on cruises are tacky. Men on cruises are fat.

*On cruises the men run around in dirty shorts and sandals*, she says. *That's the way the world is. That's what happened to the world.* The last cruise she took was nauseating. *Everyone was fat and dirty.*

Mother wants to get away but doesn't know where to go. *If I hadn't been on The Queen, I wouldn't know better*, she says.

For a couple of months, Mother hasn't paid her bills. *I've had enough. I'm finished. You can pay my bills*, she tells me. She stuffs her mail in a large envelope and sends it to California. I now have access to her bank account to pay her bills.

Because of her condition, I call every other day. Sometimes she answers the phone and hangs up. Sometimes she slams the phone in my ear. She doesn't want to talk to her imbecile brokers. She doesn't want to talk to David. If I try to calm her, she slams down the phone. Other times, we manage to have a conversation.

For years when I went to Atlanta, I'd stop briefly on my way to somewhere else. I'd stop and then continue to see my cousin Nancy in Franklin or my Aunt Bessie in Batesburg. I'd see my mother and David briefly. Mother and I would visit David in the various care homes where he lived. Homes for the mentally ill that included a wide spectrum of disorders. We'd take him grocery shopping. We'd take him out to lunch. Mother would reprimand him for the way he ate. Or the way he talked. She wanted him to say brilliant things and impress me. By the end of an hour, we were all exhausted.

After we took David back to his home, the interrogation would begin. *Isn't he handsome? Isn't he brilliant?* She apologized if he hadn't shaved. She'd tell me he usually shaved. She'd remind me of his beautiful manners. If I alluded to his sad, deteriorated state, she'd fly off the handle. She'd accuse me of wanting to hurt her. She'd nearly wreck the car. It was impossible to talk openly about David.

During these visits, Mother never asked, *Why do you have to leave so soon?* One day was enough for her, too. If my children were with me, one day was too much.

When she'd visit California, she was cold. Always cold and mostly bored. Her grandchildren took up too much of my time. *Children are overrated*, she said.

On these visits, she brought slides of her paintings. She brought them to San Francisco to show gallery owners. She was successful. Lawson's, a gallery south of Market, was happy to show her paintings. I was happy for Mother to have recognition for her paintings.

During the gallery opening, my husband John and I were at the window. We were staring out the window.

Mother asked, *What are you staring at?*

We pointed to a beautiful, rotund palm in the middle of the city.

*I hate nature*, Mother said. She was always glad to go home.

When Mother starts to fall apart, I delay going to Atlanta. From California I order her groceries and have them delivered. From California I pay her bills. If there's a problem, I try to solve it long distance. Anything to avoid going.

"You have to go," my friend Jane says.

Once said, it couldn't be plainer. I have to go.

# 27

# THE WORM AND THE WORMWOOD

From Dunwoody Nancy drives us down Peachtree Road. Through Buckhead we drive to my mother's apartment. We buzz ourselves into the building where Mother has lived for thirty-five years. Over the years, occupants have irritated her—endlessly. They buy small dogs and imagine their dogs will be content to stay alone all day. They bark from the time their owners leave until they return. Since Mother is home during the day, she hears the barking. She confronts the tenants. They deny their dogs bark. They pretend it's another dog. They say to her, "You're hearing things. My dog never barks." Mother has had a bad time with dogs and a worse time with people.

At the door, I tap softly. I turn the knob. She often leaves the door unlocked. As I slip inside, Mother lights up. She lights up like a child when she sees me. She smiles like a child. She is genuinely glad to see me. She is genuinely happy that I've come to take care of her. Despite her independence, she always wanted me to take care of her. But I never did what she wanted. I never dropped everything to take care of her. How could I? My children, their penniless fathers, my drudge jobs, my acceptance of a kind of voluntary poverty. In other words, my life safeguarded me from coming to Atlanta to take care of her. But now I'm here. I'm here to take care of her.

I've brought a bouquet. She doesn't like cut flowers. She never buys cut flowers. She knows it's a gesture. A gesture of flowers I picked up at a supermarket. Indifferently, she takes the bouquet. However, she's happy I've come.

Then Nancy appears behind me. When Nancy appears, Mother deflates. The light drains from Mother's eyes. Displeasure erases Mother's smile. She loves Nancy, but she's not glad to see her.

I know why. Mother wants me alone. She wants me to come alone. She wants my attention exclusively for her. She doesn't want anyone to distract my attention from her. But I'm afraid. She knows that, too. I'm afraid to be alone with her. She knows I've brought Nancy in case something happens. We all remember when things used to happen. When I came to visit, she would sometimes scream at me. She would sometimes scream at my children. They're her only grandchildren, and sometimes she'd viciously turn on them. Her moods are impossible to predict. That's why Nancy is with me.

Mother's living room is a baroque combo of French and Italian antiques, a Biedermeier cabinet, my grandmother's chinoiserie screens, a painted armoire for china, silver, crystal, and furs, and her own ingenious paintings. Scattered on surfaces are framed photos, a small steel sculpture, and a Sèvres bowl. There are three photographs by Mr. Skvirsky—a 1940 glamorous portrait of Mother for her engagement, a 1962 portrait of me, and a soulful portrait of David.

I remember Mr. Skvirsky. I remember his large apartment in a tall, sophisticated apartment house at the corner of Peachtree Street and Ponce de Leon Avenue. The building was brick with a curved facade, corner balconies on each floor, and two towers with belfries. A building that you'd find in New York or Paris or London. Mr. Skvirsky was Russian. Mother called him a "white Russian." I think she meant he was an aristocrat. He certainly was unusual. I remember that he loved turtles. He kept turtles in his apartment. He talked about turtles like deities.

In the first pictures Mr. Skvirsky took of me, I was wearing a white fox stole. I looked like a debutante. Then I switched to a black turtleneck sweater. Those were the pictures we all liked best. I think Mr. Skvirsky sensed I was more beatnik than deb. People were always sensing I was different—more than I recognized or admitted myself.

Mother's apartment has a careless, elegant quality like her. The wall-size windows overlook the grounds, the gardens and pool, the four-lane expressway. The room is flooded with light, but the windows are never opened. The blinds are filthy. Everything smells of mothballs.

Mother curls on the beautiful sofa covered in

Venetian red fabric with a carved walnut frame. She looks like a dragonfly. A lovely insect whose exoskeleton is collapsing. She curls around the shot silk pillows. Small and thin, she has shrunk to almost nothing. Her enormous moth-blue eyes stare out from her face. Moth-blue like star sapphires, almost gray. Her ears too are enormous. The folds of her skin are translucent, her white gossamer hair only wisps. No matter how much she eats, she can't gain weight. I've made an appointment for the doctor. But she refuses to go.

*I've given up on doctors*, she says. They've already told her that she doesn't have stomach cancer, colon cancer, ulcers, hernias, acid reflux, or any other ailments related to digestion. They believe she suffers, but they dismiss her complaints as nerves.

"I've hired Leila," I tell her. "I've hired her to clean and cook. She can check on your medication and keep you company."

"I don't want company," Mother snaps. She doesn't want anyone around. Solitude has become a habit. She doesn't want to be polite or talk to anyone. I assure her that she doesn't have to be polite, but someone needs to check on her. Someone needs to make sure she eats.

"Do you remember Leila?" I ask. "Does Leila ring a bell?"

*Nothing rings a bell*, she says. She laughs when she says, *Nothing rings a bell*.

\*

Leila took care of Nancy's mother when she lived in a nursing home. Aunt Evelyn had dementia. With dementia she was extremely cheerful. The lines of life's disappointments vanished from Evelyn's face. Yet in this new state of cheerfulness, she became unmanageable. She ran into the lobby in a negligee. The negligee was a sign of her cheerfulness and lust, but she had to be restrained. She had to be watched and sedated. That's when Leila took care of Evelyn.

A few months later, my aunt died of lymphoma. During the weeks before her death, my mother was at her side. Mother grew to love her sister again. She loved her with a fervor resurrected from their childhood. The competition for Daddy's affection was set aside or forgotten. The competition over new clothes and expensive cars was also set aside or forgotten.

*When Evelyn dies, half of me will die, too*, Mother said.

Nancy's brother Larry and my mother were often at the hospital at the same time, yelling and fighting.

"You could hear them cursing each other down the hall," Nancy said.

I had a dream that my aunt was in a coma, quiet and still, her eyes closed. In the dream, I tiptoed into the room. I stood by her bed. I stroked her hand. "Aunt Evelyn, Aunt Evelyn," I gently uttered her name. Then I told her who I was.

"You loved me," I said.

Evelyn's eyes opened, focused and clear. She'd awakened from her coma. She spoke for the first time in weeks. "I hated you," she said to me.

Even in the dream, I laughed. The morning after the dream, Nancy called to tell me that Evelyn had died.

At my aunt's funeral, Larry took charge. He and my mother sat cordially beside each other. After weeks of yelling and cursing, they were cordial. Aunt Betty was in Atlanta from New York. Mother and Evelyn used to fight over Betty, too. Nancy and her daughters came from North Carolina. Sally and her family came from Virginia. Almost all my first cousins were at Evelyn's funeral.

I offered to pick up David and bring him to the cemetery.

*David is busy!* Mother said. *He doesn't want to bother!*

He probably said he was too busy. But someone should have insisted. I should have insisted. However, it's Mother who dictates all the decisions about David. If David had come, she would have to monitor him. She would have to tell him what to wear, how to eat, what to say. It was Mother who didn't want to bother.

Our family plot in Greenwood Cemetery was bought by my grandfather for himself and my grandmother, and for their daughters and their daughters' husbands. Nevertheless, my Aunt Evelyn wasn't buried in the plot that Grandpa bought. After she and my Uncle Joe divorced, he married another woman. A young *shiksa* who converted. Uncle Joe transferred the plot for my aunt to his second wife. That's why Evelyn was buried away from her family.

After the service, we strolled through the cemetery to the Abelman plot. Grandma and Grandpa were there. Daddy and Uncle Joe were there. This marked the first time in thirty years that I'd seen Daddy's grave. When I read his name, I was heartbroken all over again.

EDWARD BRENNER

As we were looking at the gravestones, Mother said, *Evelyn could have taken my place next to Eddie. She always wanted to sleep with him. She could have slept with him for eternity.*

Daddy was dead. Evelyn was dead. Yet in her humorous way, a humor most often at the expense of someone else, Mother was working out her revenge. Or maybe not. Maybe she simply no longer cared.

After the cemetery, we convened at a restaurant for a family lunch. Then we went to Mother's apartment. We crowded into the apartment, sitting on the red sofa, the Bergère and Chippendale chairs. We told family stories. We laughed. We passed around photos. We pored over photos. Sometimes a photo made me choke. The little girl's face, who was the first version of me, especially made me choke.

A week after Evelyn died, Mother got a call from

a woman who identified herself as the daughter of Narcissus. Sixty or so years before, Narcissus took care of the three Abelman girls in their big house on Clifton Road. Narcissus's daughter had seen the obituary for Evelyn Abelman Zaglin and called to express her condolences. She also told Mother how much Narcissus loved the girls. No doubt, Narcissus spent more time with them than her own daughter. Yet Narcissus's daughter had made the effort to call.

\*

Nancy and I spend the afternoon with Mother. Mother says she wants to die. She thinks it's time for her to die. Now that she's going to die, I want to make her comfortable. I have come to Atlanta to make her comfortable. I have come to try to love her at the end.

## 28

# DAVID

David lives only a few blocks from Grant Park. As children we rarely visited the SE side of town. It was exactly opposite to our neighborhood in NW Atlanta. Only the rare visit to the famous Cyclorama in Grant Park was reason to go.

David's home is a shabby two-story apartment complex of brick buildings with weeds in between. It's called Bright Beginnings. This is where David has lived for a dozen years. Nancy and I follow him to the office. He announces his visitors at the office. He's pleased to introduce us to the staff.

"This is my sister Summer," he says. "This is my cousin Nancy."

"What a pretty sister! What a pretty cousin!"

They say how much David and I favor. David's health is wrecked. His teeth are rotten. But I'm thrilled when they say we look alike. I'm happy they recognize us as family.

We follow David outdoors to an area where he can smoke. Others are smoking, too. They're chain-smoking generic cigarettes. They sit on grimy plastic chairs in a circle, their shoulders hunched, and smoke.

David introduces us to his friends. His best friend

is also Nancy. He has known her for twenty years. They've lived together in several homes. She is blond and plump and neatly groomed. She speaks slowly in a strong Southern accent. Her skin is unwrinkled. Her face shows nothing of life's concerns. In contrast, David looks anxious and tense, the way he did as a boy. He's painfully thin and his pants too short.

Everyone at Bright Beginnings mentions David's work ethic. He works every day. He vacuums. He sweeps. He scrubs the kitchen and bathrooms. He's proud of his work. Bright Beginnings pays him a small stipend for his work. The stipend is deposited in David's bank account, where he can draw funds for extra cigarettes and Cokes. He smokes and drinks Cokes constantly. Recently, he got his teeth fixed. He opens his mouth to show me. Most of his teeth look decayed.

At Bright Beginnings, David attends crafts classes and group therapy sessions. He goes with the others on recreational outings. He doesn't like these activities. He'd rather work. He doesn't like therapy. His social worker tells me, "Your brother never opens up. He never discusses personal matters." She knows David has problems with our mother. "He never speaks about his problems," she says.

Mother used to visit David every week. Whenever she traveled out of state or out of the country, she said she couldn't be gone long because of David. On a weekly basis, she brought him his allowance. She drove him to the grocery store. She took him out to lunch. The last time Mother saw him, she came to drive him to the grocery store. They had a fight, and she attacked him. Bright Beginnings has now prohibited visits from Mother.

I already know this. When it happened, Mother reported the fight to me over the phone. She reported their exchange of words but failed to mention the attack. Or that she can no longer visit him. According to her, she told David that he needed to take care of himself.

*I'm an old woman*, she told him. *I can't drive across town to take you shopping. You're a grown man. You have to take care of yourself.*

After Mother told me about the argument, I call David to check on him. He also describes the incident. His voice quivers as he describes the fight and her attack. The description of his bloody wounds astounds me. I'm worried that he hallucinated these things. I'm worried that he had a psychotic episode.

I call David's social worker. She confirms his version. "No, it wasn't an hallucination," she says. "Your mother scratched him with her fingernails. She scratched him in the car. When he came back, he was bloody and scratched."

On our next call, I ask Mother to tell me again about her fight with David. She doesn't remember. She's forgotten. She's unaware of the wreckage in her wake. She blames Bright Beginnings.

*Social workers make too much of everything,* she says. *Social workers want to control David.*

I agree with Mother that David should be more independent. I agree that he can take care of his own needs. I suggest she give him a credit card. With a credit card, they can avoid contact. With a credit card, he can withdraw money by himself. Or charge necessities to the card. He can take the bus to the grocery store. He can use the credit card for food, clothing, cigarettes, and Cokes. He won't have to depend on her.

"It'll be good for both of you," I say.

"What if he overspends?"

"You can put a limit on his spending," I say. Thinking, cigarettes, Cokes, socks, these things cost almost nothing.

Mother thinks $30 a month is adequate.

"No, it's not," I say. "Cat food costs more than that."

"Then how much?"

"$100," I tell her.

After Mother gives David a credit card, it's not necessary for her to visit. She's relieved not to visit. They're both relieved.

Although David is glad to see Nancy and me, he quickly gets nervous.

"I can't spend much time," he says. "I have to get back to work."

He doesn't want us to take him to lunch or grocery shopping. He makes excuses. He has to do laundry. He has to clean the bathrooms. When he says good-bye, he asks me for money. After he takes the bills, he furtively hides them inside his pocket.

Before we leave, I tell him that Mother is ill. I tell him that she's probably dying. I ask him, "Do you want to see Mother?"

David doesn't want to see her. After all the years of their interdependence, which is his whole lifetime, I'm surprised. I also respect his decision. I know she hurt him deeply. She hurt all of us, but he's the one who suffered most.

As for Mother, her fury is nearly mystical. Mythical and mystical. She spent much of her adult life being furious—furious about nearly everything. It was her life force. If she weren't furious, she couldn't get out of bed. That's why Evelyn's death was significant. When her sister died, she lost her best enemy. Whenever she mentions Evelyn now, words of sisterly love pour out of her.

Mother is depleted. She's physically and mentally depleted. She has little energy to do anything. The fury-driven years are nearly over.

## 29

## FAMILY JEWELS

I return to Atlanta the next month. My daughter Joanna meets me in Atlanta. Joanna lives in New York. She is twenty and goes to college in New York. She flies to Atlanta and meets me. Nancy drives down from her home in the mountains. We all stay at Nancy's daughter's condo in suburban Dunwoody. Joanna has come to Atlanta to help me. I want us to clean Mother's apartment. I want us to vacuum, sweep, dust, wash, wipe the blinds, scrape, and throw out old food.

Mother is worse. She doesn't get dressed. She doesn't remember to eat. She has cut her arm. Her arm has a gash. She doesn't remember what happened or how long ago. The blood is mostly in the bathroom.

*I knocked my arm against the towel rack*, she says.

During these weeks, Leila has come. At first, Mother wouldn't let Leila inside the apartment. Mother told her, *Go away*. But Leila stood outside Mother's door until she opened it. Whenever Leila comes, she tidies up. She cooks and does laundry. Mother didn't want her to come, but now she looks forward to Leila. She likes Leila's company. Leila is talkative and sympathetic.

Mother loves to see me clean. She marvels at how hard I work. She can't understand how I became such a good worker. I grew up having to do nothing. Neither make a bed nor wash a dish. But I turned out to be a very good worker.

For years Mother has been cleaning her apartment. She has been cutting her hair. Her apartment is filthy. Her hair looks like a lunatic cut it. She thinks it's chic. She thinks her style can carry it off. She'd prefer to have a house cleaner and go to the beauty parlor, but she doesn't want to spend the money.

When we arrive at the apartment, Mother makes Joanna turn around and around. She wants to inspect every inch of her. She's astonished by Joanna's painted nails, her clever haircut, her hip clothes. Joanna laughs with Mother. She cleans with me and humors Mother. It's a good day, cleaning and laughing.

When Mother used to visit us in California, she'd sit in the corner and watch me work. I lived in small cottages or small apartments with two children. From her seat, she watched me cook, wash, and clean. She'd say, *I wish there was something I could do to help.* Repeatedly, she'd say, *I wish I could do something.*

When Mother would visit, my young son Felix would imitate her Southern accent. When he was very young, he'd wave a make-believe cigarette between his fingers and say, "I wish thar was a way I could heelp."

I never asked her to help. I knew she didn't want to help. She felt badly she didn't want to help. But not so badly to clear the table or play with the kids.

Joanna is a good helper. Although she has been a recipient of Mother's wrath, she treats her grandmother with great tenderness. Mother admires the way my children turned out. She can't believe the way they turned out. With my life, she doesn't understand how it happened. But she worries about Joanna. She nags me about Joanna. She wants Joanna to meet nice people. She wants her to go to a school where there are nice boys she can marry. She worries that Joanna is dating boys who are beneath her. She knows Joanna's boyfriends come from poor circumstances. She knows they grew up in the projects. She doesn't want Joanna to do what I did. Or live like I did.

I've met a few of these boyfriends. From Mother I learned to keep my mouth shut. Mother never kept her mouth shut. She always criticized the men in my life. Criticism is not a good strategy. Keeping your mouth shut is better.

*You need to get married and set a good example for Joanna*, Mother says.

*You made your life too hard. You had to work all the time*, Mother says.

She doesn't understand why I made things hard. She doesn't understand why I didn't marry a rich man. Maybe I was inspired by my Aunt Bessie. She always worked. She seemed happy to work. She didn't complain about working. She was a role model for me. A contrast to my mother and aunt who had everything done for them and always complained.

*Something is wrong with you*, Mother says.

I did set a bad example for my kids. However, my choices weren't bad for me. I think my choices made me strong. I think they reflected my beliefs. Despite my romantic fantasies, I didn't want anybody to take care of me. Or maybe I didn't trust anybody to take care of me. Whatever the reasons, obvious or obscure, I learned to take care of myself. My joke is that I've been downwardly mobile since I left home. My other joke is that Daddy told me I could do anything—and I ended up doing everything.

While I'm scrubbing the tub, Mother and Joey watch TV.

*Where's that bitch?* Mother asks her.

Later Joey tells me, "Your mom called you a bitch."

I laugh, but Joanna is shocked. I fly in from California. I fly Joanna down from New York. We spend the day cleaning Mother's apartment—and she calls me a *bitch*. Mother likes to say the unexpected. She likes to make jokes at someone else's expense. I'm used to it. Despite what Mother says, I know she appreciates our effort. She's happy we've come to be with her.

Throughout the afternoon, when we're not cleaning, we sit on the sofa with Mother. I'd like her to move somewhere safe. A place where she has help. A place where she's not alone.

*Now that the apartment is clean, there's no reason to move*, she says.

*Why did your father kill himself?* she asks.
*What went wrong?* she wonders.
*How did he ruin his life?* She wants me to explain.
"I don't know, I don't know," I say.
*What will happen to David when I die?* she asks.
"I'll move him to California," I assure her.

Mother is happy that I'll move him. She has designated a lawyer as David's guardian, but she's relieved that I'll take care of David. I've told her for years that I'd take care of him. I've already asked him to move. I've already looked for a place. My friend John Badanes has a schizophrenic brother who lives in a care home in Berkeley. That's where I hope David can live, too.

"If I can't find a place, David can live with me," I say.
*You're ridiculous,* Mother says.

She doesn't want me to take on the burden of David. She thinks it's too much. He has been a burden in her life. She doesn't want to pass the burden of David to me. She only wants me to find him a decent place to live and visit him.

Mother reminds me about her safe deposit box. She reminds me fifteen times. She reminds me how much her furniture is worth. Especially the inlaid Biedermeier cabinet. She sent a photo and description of it to Sotheby's, which they appraised at $75,000. She tells me as soon as she dies, I have to remove it from the apartment to avoid an estate tax. She tells me fifteen times.

Through the years, I've asked her how much money

she has, but she never answers. *You'll think I'm rich,* she says. *I'm not rich. I can't afford new clothes. I can't afford a nice trip.*

Mother turns to the television. There's a movie with Gene Kelly on TV. She hates Gene Kelly. She says it fifteen times. She hates what's happening in the government. She hates George W. Bush. She thinks he and his cronies are ruining the world. She thinks the world is ending.

*I'm glad I won't live to see it,* she says.

Mother says she'd like to kill the President. It's her greatest wish. Her last wish. She wants to shoot him. She thinks that she'd be successful because no one would suspect her. After she shot him, then the Secret Service would shoot her. Mother thinks hers would be a heroic death. A service to mankind.

"Do you still want to be cremated?" I ask.

Yes, she wants to be cremated. When she first mentioned it a dozen years ago, I asked if I should take her ashes to Paris. She accused me of using her death as an excuse to go to Paris. Instead, she told me, *Drop them at the Guggenheim. If they won't take my paintings when I'm alive, they can have me when I'm dead.*

"What would you like me to do with the ashes?" I ask.

She asks what I want.

"I want to bury you next to Daddy and your parents."

Mother says she doesn't care. *Do whatever you want,* she says.

After we finish cleaning, Mother asks Joanna to get her jewelry box. The white leather cube, embossed in gold with Mother's initials R.A.B. Of her many glamorous things, I always thought the most glamorous was Mother's white leather luggage.

*I want to give you a piece of jewelry*, she says to Joey.

She asks Joanna to sit beside her. She wants them to examine her jewelry together. From the box, she lifts up a heavy gold braided chain.

*This is the chain your mother wants, but she can't have it. It's too good to give her.*

Too good to give Joanna or me.

She lifts up a diamond and sapphire brooch. *This is too good to give you, too.*

She dangles a strand of amber and jade beads. *You can't have these. They're too good.*

The pearls, she can't give them away. Or the necklace made of glass birds. Or the lapis choker.

Mother is disappointed. *There's nothing in the box I can give you*, she tells Joanna.

Finally, she finds a pair of costume earrings. These she can part with. These aren't too good to give away.

## 30

# THE LAST STOP

In early August, Leila tries to open Mother's door. It's locked. Leila knocks. But Mother can barely move. She can barely get out of bed. When Mother finally opens the door, she collapses.

Leila calls an ambulance. Piedmont Hospital is not far. It's only a few blocks from Mother's apartment house. I call the hospital. I talk to Mother. I talk to the doctors. The doctors say they don't know what's wrong. They're conducting tests. They don't think she's dying. They don't think it's an emergency.

On Saturday I arrive in Atlanta. Mother is very content. She's in a private room. She's happy to have nothing to do. She's fed and bathed. She sleeps and reads. She watches TV. She looks beautiful—ethereal and beautiful. Her face is nearly unlined, her lips pink, her choppy hair combed.

She wants to know. *Am I dying?* Whenever a doctor comes into the room, she asks, *Am I dying?*

If he says he doesn't know, she gets upset.

*I want to die*, she says with great sincerity. *Bring me a poison pill or a gun*, she tells the nurses.

The doctors and nurses think she's kidding. They tell her things will get better. They assure her she's going to be fine. The more they assure, the angrier Mother gets. She doesn't want to get better. But Mother's honesty goes against their training. They're trained to reassure and comfort everyone.

From what I've said, you may have the wrong impression of my mother. I've revealed the most difficult and disagreeable things about her. In fact, she has irresistible charm and wit. The doctors and nurses adore her. They respect her honesty.

A nurse asks if she prefers Rita or Mrs. Brenner. *I prefer darling*, Mother says.

I spend the next few days at the hospital. Sometimes Nancy comes to the hospital, but Mother doesn't want to see Nancy. Nancy waits for me in the lobby. Mother doesn't want to see David. I offer to pick up David and bring him to the hospital, but she doesn't want to see him. She doesn't want to see her sister Betty. Betty calls me to ask if she can visit. She asks what day she should fly from Chapel Hill to Atlanta.

"It would be good to see your sister," I say to Mother. "Betty cries whenever she calls."

*She can cry at my funeral*, Mother says.

She and Betty used to have a good relationship. When Betty lived in New York, Mother stayed at Betty's apartment on West End Avenue. Over the years, Mother and Aunt Evelyn competed for Betty's love. Like they competed for Daddy's. But Mother got tired of Betty. Betty's medication for epilepsy made her a little slow.

Mother lost patience. She got angry. Whatever the reason, she decided Betty was stupid. That's typically what Mother concluded about everyone.

Mother doesn't want to see anyone but me. She wants me to sit on the bed by her side and talk. She wants me to answer her questions.

*Do you believe in God?* She wants to know. *How can one man do all that?*

*How did your father die?* Then she remembers. *He killed himself.* She remembers but doesn't know why.

*I wish I'd been more loving to your father.* She regrets she wasn't more loving.

*He was a genius,* she reminds me. *He turned down MIT.* She wants to know what was wrong with him.

Mother only breaks down on the subject of David. Her face shrivels. Tears leak from her enormous eyes. *David was a curse on my life,* she cries.

I'm shocked. Her words are a shock. *DAVID WAS A CURSE ON MY LIFE!* Yes, a burden and a big responsibility—but a *curse*? Mother spent her life trying to validate David. She ruled David's life. She mediated everything in his life. It was impossible to be close to David without her mediation and manipulation. Because of this, I chose to leave David alone. I chose to leave them to each other. I rejected her fantasies about him. And now she calls him a *curse.* Everything I thought I knew about my family flips upside down. Calling him a *curse* means David was deserted by everyone, even his mother.

After ten days in the hospital, there's a diagnosis.

*Will I die soon?* Mother wants to know. *Give me the good news!*

"Mrs. Brenner, you have a bone marrow disease. Your bone marrow has hardened, and parts of your liver and spleen have hardened, too."

The disease is myelofibrosis. A rare type of blood cancer in which the bone marrow is replaced by fibrous scar tissue. It's a form of chronic leukemia, fatal and incurable. It could account for her years of abdominal pain.

Mother is delighted with these dire pronouncements. She raises her fist in a gesture of victory. She only wants to know, *How long will it take?*

The doctors predict a couple of months, more or less. But it's unpredictable.

*Can't it be sooner?* she asks.

They don't know. Except for a transfusion, there's nothing more the doctors can do. The transfusion might delay her death, but Mother doesn't want any delays.

It's time for her to leave the hospital. I have to decide where she'll go. If I take her home, I'll have to hire help. Leila is sweet, but she's old and undependable. She's too weak to lift Mother. If I take her home, I'll have to rent a hospital bed and other equipment. Also, Mother's home is cluttered. Not only the clutter of things but the clutter of her life. It's not a peaceful place. Despite our efforts at cleaning, it's dirty.

The hospital's social worker suggests hospice.

Mother's condition qualifies for hospice. I tell Mother I'm going out to look at hospices. She's unfamiliar with the term.

"A hospice is a place where you can die," I say.

*Good,* she says. She's eager to get on with it.

There's a lovely hospice near Buckhead. It's quiet. Its rooms are spacious. It's clean but not sterile. There are French doors, a garden, fountains, and lush foliage. It has the quality of a resort. The last resort.

I decide to move Mother to the hospice. There's a vacant room. She can move today. I ask what I should bring to the hospice. Then I return to her apartment. The rooms already feel lifeless because she'll never see them again. The red sofa, the Bergère chairs, the silver and Sèvres china, the paintings and books, the brass beds, the closets full of mothballs and designer clothes are all lifeless without Mother.

I pack a small bag. I put in pajamas, a jacquard satin robe, her slippers, and Lancôme night cream.

Mother is transferred by ambulance from the hospital to the hospice. I've gone ahead by car. I'm waiting for Mother. When she arrives, I walk beside the gurney. She's wheeled down the hall to her room. The walls are buttery yellow. The paisley bedspread matches the drapes. The bed faces the French doors, framed by flowers in bloom.

Mother enters the room. She nods approvingly. *What a beautiful room! If only the ceiling was higher,* she says. Rather than a complaint, it's an observation. She's correct. Everything is diminished because of the ceiling height.

An orderly comes to help my mother. He calls her, "My little lady." He says it several times, "My little lady, my little lady."

*I wish I could get comfortable,* Mother says over and over.

She tosses her tiny body around. She wrestles with the sheets. She can't get comfortable. The nurses adjust the bed. They bring extra pillows for her back and knees. Nothing works. The only comfort is a pill. Mother is given a pill to sleep.

When I arrive in the morning, Mother is waking up. When her eyes open fully, she sees me and says, *You said I was going to die here.*

She thinks I've betrayed her. Her shrill voice is filled with harsh and familiar accusations.

*Didn't you say I'd die here?*

"You are going to die here," I say.

She summons the strength to shout. *Why aren't I dead?*

"I didn't promise you'd die overnight," I say.

Raising her hand, she pleads to heaven, *God please, let me die.*

# 31

# FAREWELL

I kiss Mother on the cheek. She doesn't like to kiss. She usually waits to be kissed. If she does the kissing, the effort is pro forma. When you kiss her, she only tolerates it. Then she takes a tissue and wipes her face. It's not entirely lack of affection. It's partly habit. Her mother did the same thing. But Anna, my grandmother, explained that it was because of germs. Grandma had a phobia of germs. Maybe because she grew up in New York when epidemics killed a lot of children. With Mother I sense it's something more than germs.

I kiss Mother good-bye. We look into each other's eyes. I find mine swimming inside hers. My eyes are tadpoles swimming inside the blue and white of her eyes. I cry and hold her hand, which is lighter than a twig.

"I love you," I tell her. Although damaged and wasted, the love is genuine.

*You've been a wonderful daughter*, she tells me. I don't contradict her although I've not been *wonderful*. Dutiful, but not wonderful.

"You've been a wonderful mother," I assure her.

These are courtesies. These are formalities. These are also expressions of reconciliation. She gave me life and whatever else she could, bad and good. I gave her disappointments and anxiety. *Tsuris*, they say in Yiddish. Maybe also a little joy and pride. We both believe we tried. No matter what else, at the end we profess our love.

Mother is not only resigned to death but brave. She teaches me how to die. Her life lessons were not so helpful, many of them terrifying, but her lesson about death is a great gift. She has looked on it without illusions. All the former illusions of her life, the tragedies of my father and brother, her struggles with money and status, her achievements and failures as an artist, are overtaken by these final moments. There is nothing left to count or calculate except a few breaths—a few inhalations and exhalations. She is face to face with the end of her life. She doesn't cower or shirk.

When I get to the airport, I believe I'll see my mother again. The doctors have told me she will live weeks or months. The hospice has said, "Go, there's time."

I'm taking the time. I'm going home for a few days. I'm going back to manage a few things at work. Then I'll return. At the airport, I call my children. I call Felix in San Francisco. I call Joanna in New York. I'm sobbing.

My children are a great comfort. They have nothing to say, but their presence on the telephone pours into me. One part of me, the last of my two parents, pours out of me. And the other part, my children, pours into me. I feel like a vessel, part empty, part full. The pouring is continuous. It has always been continuous. The moment I was born, the filling and the emptying began. It began with my parents, and now their part is nearly over. The struggles of love and discontent between us are nearly over. There is nothing to be done. Nothing to do about my mother's death. Nothing to do about her life. We have nearly reached the end of the road. Soon, she'll be dead. Soon, we'll all be dead.

# 32

# DEATH'S BUSINESS

My cousin Sally is visiting Atlanta from her home in Virginia. Sally is Nancy and Larry's younger sister. Sally grew up with us in Atlanta. Sally goes to see my mother at the hospice. She holds Mother's hand. She murmurs comfort. She's the last family member to see Mother.

Mother dies a few days after I return to California. I leave on Saturday, and she dies on Tuesday. It's fortunate how quickly she dies. She doesn't suffer from pain. She doesn't linger. She willfully dies as she willfully managed so many things in life.

I call the hospice every day. From work I call the hospice. On Tuesday when I call, they tell me that my mother just died. They find it uncanny that I should call at the very moment of my mother's death.

"Your mother just died," they say.

Her death is a terrible blow. I'm surprised it's a blow. I was expecting her to die but not today. Not August 21, 2001.

The hospice will have the body removed and sent to the crematorium. The funeral home will pick up the ashes and keep them until the funeral. I have made these arrangements in advance. These things have been arranged, but now there are more things to arrange—the funeral and funeral notice, discussions with the funeral home, discussions with a community rabbi, notification to relatives, legal and financial responsibilities, and of course, David.

Mother has a lawyer whom I met in June. Mother's lawyer is David's legal guardian. I met with him to discuss the terms of Mother's will. David's portion of the estate is to be left in trust. But since David is a ward of the state, I was concerned that his benefits might be jeopardized. Mother's lawyer wasn't concerned. He assured me, "The law protects David's trust."

When my mother's lawyer and I first meet, we are cordial. He sits behind his big desk and exudes cordiality. His well-scrubbed face and scrutinizing button eyes, his thin swept-back hair and bow tie make him look Southern. But like so many others in Atlanta, he's a transplant. He's from Milwaukee. He once clerked for my close friend Laura Chester's father, a prominent lawyer in Milwaukee. That I knew George Chester made him very cordial.

Mother and I discuss changing her will. I speak to Mother about changing her will. I suggest she change the equal proportion of inheritance between David and me. I make the suggestion because David's care is guaranteed by the state. She has my promise that if David needs anything, I'll provide it.

Mother approves of my suggestion. She sees the logic

of my suggestion. She thinks it's fair. But she doesn't contact her lawyer. I contact him. Throughout the summer, I leave messages at his office. But the will is never changed. I don't know why he never helped my mother change her will. Maybe he was lazy, or thought I had bad intentions, or wanted to remain David's guardian.

In the end, Mother's lawyer and I fight. At the end of my mother's life, we fight over her will. He yells at me, "I'm not your lawyer. Find another lawyer." It's trite the way we fight.

In the end, it's demeaning to argue over money. At the same time, it's funny because haggling over the money of the dead is part of the human comedy.

Mother's lawyer and I are on bad terms. It's necessary for me to find my own lawyer. I'm glad to pay someone to talk to my mother's lawyer. I need my own lawyer to talk to my mother's lawyer because I can't stand him. I can't stand that he thinks I would do something dishonorable. I can't stand that despite my mother's wishes, he refused to change her will.

My son Felix helps. He's a young lawyer. Through his connections, he helps me find a local estate lawyer. My new lawyer knows my mother's lawyer. My new lawyer once worked with my mother's lawyer. They're chummy.

Mother's will allows me to fire David's guardian and appoint myself as guardian. That's the first thing I do. I fire my mother's lawyer. "It's not a problem," my lawyer tells me. Apparently, Mother's lawyer is relieved he won't have to visit or check on David. That now falls to me. I'm glad it falls to me. I'm glad to take care of David.

According to Jewish custom, you are expected to bury the dead quickly. According to Jewish custom, cremation is not allowed. Fortunately, the funeral home, the rabbi, and the cemetery don't care if Mother is cremated. They don't care if I want to bury her ashes in the Abelman family plot.

I arrange the funeral for September. September gives everyone time to make travel arrangements. I arrange two funerals. The hospice offers me their chapel. The hospice chapel will host a public funeral on Saturday. There will be a notice in the newspaper. Afterwards David and I will host a lunch for the family. We will host it in a restaurant at Lenox Square. The restaurant is not far from the hospice. That's what I arrange. The second funeral will take place on Sunday at the grave site. On Sunday there will be a family service with a rabbi.

I'm glad to do these things for my mother. I can honor her without her criticism or disapproval. I don't have to listen to her say, *Don't bother*. Or accuse me of trying to attract attention. Or wasting my inheritance. I can do things the way I want to.

Like all the hospice rooms, the chapel is well-appointed. It's flooded with sunlight. The chaplain is young and cheerful. He tells me, "I'd like to sing at the service." I think it's appropriate that he sing. Mother herself loved to sing. She knew the lyrics to many standards. When I was a child, she tinkled them on the piano. She taught me the lyrics, and I also memorized them on my own. I learned them from listening to the LPs at our house. I too loved to sing along and dance to these songs. Maybe my happiest memory of Mother is driving with her around Saint Simon's Island and singing Broadway show tunes.

The chaplain has an earnest voice. The song he has chosen to sing is "Bridge over Troubled Water." His choice of song embarrasses me. It's a cloying song. And whatever meaning it might have to my generation, it would have meant nothing to Mother. However, it would have made her laugh. Howl is more like it. I nearly howl myself. But I resist giving in to laughter. If I start, I'll lose control. If I look at Nancy, I'll lose control. Nancy and I have a history of laughing and losing control.

After the chaplain sings, he says a prayer. I have asked him to choose prayers that are spiritual, not religious. I've asked him not to mention Jesus. I don't want anything to sound churchy. The chaplain leads us in prayer and then opens the ceremony to participation. We are able to speak. This is the moment in the service to speak.

I thank everyone for coming. I thank my fiancé Michael, my children, and my cousins. Mother's sister Betty has driven from Chapel Hill with her children. My cousin Gail has flown in from New Jersey. There is

Leila and her husband, a few of Mother's old friends, and a neighbor from my mother's apartment house. After thirty-five years of living there, only one neighbor comes.

My friend Moe Slotin promised to come from Savannah. He planned to drive from Savannah to Atlanta. For years Moe and I have been great friends. Since he moved from New York to Savannah, I don't see him. I used to see him on my trips to New York. Or on tour when he worked as a sound engineer for rock bands and came to San Francisco. After his daughter was born, they moved out of New York. Moe grew up in Savannah. Our parents knew each other. When I was a girl, I knew his aunt. But Moe and I didn't meet until we were grown. When I met Moe, it was like meeting a lost cousin. He and I grew close. It surprises me when Moe doesn't show up. He's a person who always does what he says.

All of us stay at the same hotel in Buckhead. We're glad to be together. It's also wonderful for David. David has been cut off from the family for decades. Except for Nancy, Ronnie, and Evans, David hasn't seen our cousins since he got sick. After the service, David and I treat everyone to lunch. David is happy to be with us. An evil spell has lifted—and now he can be with us.

Sunday is the religious service. The grave is open. The ashes are in an urn. The rabbi makes the traditional Hebrew prayers. The rabbi gives a sermon. Although he never met my mother, he has prepared a sermon. The day before the service, he came to the hotel. We talked for a long time. We talked for two hours. He not only spoke to me but to my children, too. I like the rabbi. I like the thoughtful questions he asked me. Although he never met my mother, the sermon is extremely thoughtful. It seems as if he knew her. He speaks familiarly about her life. He speaks of the difficulties of her life. He doesn't prettify the difficulties. He doesn't prettify her temperament. He speaks about the hardships of an artist. He speaks of how art connects difficulties with resolution. He makes a tribute to Mother as an artist. It's a beautiful sermon.

When the rabbi finishes, the urn of ashes is lowered. The urn of ashes is buried next to Daddy. But not all the ashes. The funeral director saves a small bag of ashes for me. After the ashes are lowered, everyone at the service throws dirt into the hole. This is a Jewish custom. It's a primitive feeling to throw dirt into a hole. A feeling so deep that it turns into knowledge—profound knowledge. A feeling that connects us to our foremothers and forefathers. It connects us to ancient times. Humans have been throwing dirt into the holes of graves since they began to bury their dead. After we throw dirt, we place rocks on the graves of our family. Buried around us are Grandpa, Grandma, Uncle Joe, Daddy, and now Mother. Only Aunt Evelyn is missing. Each of us has picked up a rock from the ground to put on our family graves. This is a Jewish custom, too.

After Mother's funeral, we leave the cemetery. We take David home to Bright Beginnings. We take Felix and Joanna to the hotel so they can pack. They're leaving on afternoon flights. Felix is returning to San Francisco and Joanna to New York. The cousins are leaving, too.

I will stay in Atlanta. Michael will stay in Atlanta. He will help me sort through Mother's things. He will help me clean, sort, pack, and ship. There is much to be done. I am grateful that Michael can help. I didn't ask him to stay. I didn't ask him to help. It's hard sometimes for me to ask for help, but he could tell I needed him to stay.

## 33

# A WEEK OF CRISES

On Monday I call the appraiser, which is required by law. Mother has impressed upon me how much her furnishings are worth. The European antiques, the *grise* panels of *putti* (dated 1806), the crystal, the silver, the china. I call a moving company to estimate the cost of shipping the things I want to keep. I call an antique dealer on Buford Highway. I've spoken to him about my mother's most ornate things. Whatever he doesn't take will go to an auction house. Also, on the list is the cable company, the condo, the car. By the end of the day, we've made a good start.

On Tuesday we leave the hotel and drive to the nearest Waffle House. We plan to eat breakfast at a Waffle House en route to Mother's apartment. As we drive, a radio newscaster shouts, "A plane has crashed into the tower!" Her description is confusing. She explains she's on a bridge. I envision a tower on another bridge. I envision a plane crashing on its way to land at the airport.

"We can't make out what's happening. But a plane has crashed into the tower!"

I don't understand that *tower* means one of the Twin Towers. But as we walk into the Waffle House, a second plane hits another tower. It's not the tower of a bridge.

It's the second of the Twin Towers. Instantly, it's clear. Instantly, we know it's sabotage.

All day we listen to the news. While cleaning Mother's apartment, we listen to the news. It's awful to sift through Mother's life and listen to the news. We try calling Felix in California. We can't get through. We try calling Joanna in New York. It's impossible to get through. The lines are jammed or communication cut off, we don't know.

When we finally reach Joanna, she's all right. From her school in Brooklyn, she has seen one of the Twin Towers fall, but she's all right. Thousands of shreds of paper have drifted over Brooklyn. The fire's strong acrid smell is everywhere. But she's all right.

When Michael and I return to the hotel, all we do is watch TV. We sit in the lobby with other hotel guests and watch TV. Everyone is stunned. I take the car and drive to Loehmann's, a discount designer clothing store. As a distraction, I scan the racks of clothes. It briefly silences the barrage of news. It briefly interrupts the replays of death and destruction—the falling towers, the monstrous clouds of thick dust, the masses of people running for their lives, the panic and sorrow. Momentarily, I forget the death grip of my own personal life and the nation's.

During the following days, Michael and I sort through Mother's things. I plan to give away the books I don't want. We must locate a donation box for books. I plan to take her clothes to a thrift shop or consignment store in Buckhead. I plan to pick up her dry cleaning. I don't have a claim ticket. It helps that I can identify myself with the same last name.

"My mother died," I explain to the dry cleaner. "I'm from California, and my mother died." It upsets me to tell him that Mother is dead. I could have abandoned her dry cleaning, but I want to be thorough. Being thorough is a distraction. It keeps me busy.

The apartment reeks of mothballs. Mother's clothes reek of mothballs. Mother kept her closets saturated with mothballs. Moths in Georgia are voracious. Mother also painted her paintings in the apartment. The apartment often reeked of mothballs, paint, and turpentine. Myelofibrosis is a rare leukemia. Causes include petrochemicals, such as benzene or toluene. Mothballs are commonly made of naphthalene or paradichlorobenzene, both toxic. Toluene is found in lacquers, paint thinners, paints, and adhesives. Mother's two greatest creative expressions—painting and clothes—may have caused or contributed to her suffering and death.

I call a realtor. I have to sell the apartment. I want to sell it quickly, but the market is slow. I call cable TV, the telephone company, and the other utilities to close Mother's accounts. Before I contact Mother's brokers and banks, I have to order copies of the death certificate. I have to prove she's dead. I have to prove that I'm the executrix.

Except for some stock certificates, most of Mother's money is in managed accounts. When I visit her brokers, they offer their condolences.

One wants to tell me stories about my mother. "She used to call me a big baby," he says. "She'd *wawa wawa* into the phone and call me a big baby."

He pretends to be amused. Or maybe it's only amusing now that he doesn't have to put up with her. I'm sure she harassed him. I'm sure she tried to make him feel incompetent and small. But I resent his telling me. I think it's rude for him to tell me. He knows nothing about my relationship with my mother. She used to say her brokers were stupid. It's stupid of him to tell me.

The appraiser comes to appraise everything in the apartment. It takes him hours. He describes each item in writing. He writes elaborate descriptions in a tiny spidery script and jots down his appraisal in a notebook. Mother's furnishings are not *worth a fortune*. Most of them are copies. As for the *grise* panels of *putti* (dated 1806) that once hung in a house built by Christopher Wren, the appraiser says, "The date was changed." It's not an authentic date. He guesses they were painted in 1906, the 9 later changed to 8. The appraiser says, "They're valuable but not worth a fortune." He inspects the Bergère chairs, the Chippendale chairs, the ormolu chest and side tables, the pair of Chinoiserie screens, and Mother's ivory inlaid cabinet, which she said Sotheby's assessed at $75,000. The appraiser shows me the drawers in the cabinet. He tells me the pegs in the drawers indicate that the piece is a copy. He guesses that it was built by Italian cabinetmakers after World War II. He agrees that it's beautiful but not *worth a fortune*. As for my grandmother's ball-in-claw Chippendale chairs, they aren't genuine either. The appraiser estimates the entirety at $10,000.

I'm relieved the estate won't be taxed. But I'm also disappointed for Mother. I'm amused and disappointed. I wonder if she was duped by fake pedigrees for these antiques. Or paid low prices and later grew convinced that she owned a household of treasures.

Mother was buried on Sunday. The Twin Towers fell on Tuesday. We're scheduled to leave on Friday. Friday is the first day that flights will be allowed to leave Atlanta.

We are told to arrive several hours before departure time. The airport is crowded and chaotic. Nothing is normal at the airport. Every seat in every waiting area is occupied. People are sitting in every seat or camped on the floor. Most, or maybe all of them, have been in the airport since Tuesday—sitting, eating, sleeping, and waiting for flights to take them from Atlanta.

Our plane is delayed. There aren't enough flight attendants. They have to find them elsewhere. They have to fly them to Atlanta. Pilots too have been stranded around the country. It's highly disorganized. It takes a long time to find enough personnel for our plane. Our departure is delayed five hours. When we finally board the plane, I'm more nervous than usual. I ask a stewardess if she's nervous. She hasn't flown since Monday. None of them has flown on an official flight since Monday. This is their first official flight. I go back to the galley and talk to the stewardesses. They try to sound reassuring, but everyone is nervous. I'm nervous, and they're nervous, too.

## 34

# THE WRITTEN WORD

The most surprising of my mother's possessions is a document. I find it inside an envelope, marked in Mother's nearly illegible hand.

*LETTER FROM MASS GEN—*
*OPEN ONLY IF NECESSARY*

In black pen is scrawled <u>*HORRIBLE!*</u> and underlined several times. Inside the envelope are records from Children's Medical Center in Boston dated April 1952. Attached to the records is my mother's request for these documents and an acknowledgment of her request dated August 1988. I recollect that Mother also attempted to seal these documents legally, but there's no indication if she succeeded.

I recall when Mother and Daddy took David to Boston. I was seven. They left me with Mae, the practical nurse who took care of David after he was born. Joseph Patterson, our pediatrician in Atlanta, recommended that my parents take David to Massachusetts General for tests. Dr. Patterson is Daddy's first cousin. He and Daddy grew up together in Hendersonville. Daddy always called him "Dodie." We call him Uncle Dodie. Uncle Dodie told my parents that he lacked the expertise to evaluate David. That's why he advised them to go to Boston.

The first document is from the Neurological Division IX service. David's name is misspelled *Brennan*.

INFORMANT: Parents who are interested and reliable; however, they do not give a very detailed or coherent history.

[David was] born October 24, 1949 following a full-term, normal pregnancy . . . [and] required 15 minutes resuscitation with external stimulation, aspiration, mouth-to-mouth breathing, oxygen as well as chloramine: and for approximately 4 hours after birth there was hyperpnea with sneezing and some grunting with expiration . . . baby was bottle fed . . . mother states that she thought the child was premature because he seemed so small.

[David's] development is slower than normal for his age . . . only in the past 2 to 3 months has he said a few words . . . not toilet trained at all . . . extremely restless, shows little interest in toys or playmates . . . forever pulling at the mother's skirt and demanding attention.

[David has] a sibling, girl age 7 years, living and well, said to be somewhat "precocious."

This is a pale, rather peculiar-looking child in that he has a small face and a rather pointed head and is extremely restless.

IMPRESSION: MENTAL RETARDATION.
DIAGNOSIS: MENTAL RETARDATION. 000-X90. DWARFISM, MILD. 010-076.

X-RAY REPORT: Examination of the skull shows no definite variation from the normal.

PSYCHOLOGICAL EVALUATION:
During his stay on the Ward, David seemed to be very immature, a rather hectic little boy, who doesn't talk, but jabbers and grunts some. . . . The child while extremely active and demanding with his mother, settled down considerably while here, and seemed content enough to sit for quite some time, placing and displacing blocks from one place to the next. His father described more constructive activities at home, such as occasionally helping to make a bed, etc. . . . The child at home is taken care of by a nurse, who does not find him especially difficult, while his mother feels incapable of coping with him, or of giving much of any useful information about him.

Attached to the medical reports is a letter dated April 21, 1952 from a doctor in Boston to Uncle Dodie, our pediatrician in Atlanta.

Dear Dr. Patterson:

[It was] quite obvious that the child was extraordinarily small. . . . His behavior was quite primitive . . . mostly in pushing a cart about the ward, which he did in quite a blundering sort of way, going straight ahead until it ran into a bed or something, and then backing off and starting in another direction until he hit something. . . . [It was] obvious he understood language. . . . [He was] pathetic in his desire to hang onto somebody's hand for some sort of moral support. . . . [He seemed to be] under twenty months rather than one of two and one-half years.

[The] mother, I think, is quite unable to grasp anything except the most concrete statements. I told her, for instance, that at this time I would be utterly unable to make any long range forecast about this child's future, and she immediately countered by saying, "Well, will he be happy at eighteen?" I feel that her mental processes are probably quite limited and that she has been a large factor in producing the emotional situation in this child. . . . I think all of us who saw him here felt that his eventual outlook was not very good, but none of us felt we could guess whether he would have an I.Q. of 50 or 85.

*[The] mother, I think, is quite unable to grasp anything except the most concrete statements. I feel that her mental processes are probably quite limited and that she has been a large factor in producing the emotional situation in this child.*

I'm sad for my mother. I sympathize with her fury and frustration. And her determination to prove the doctors wrong. I also find their statements callous. *[David is] pathetic in his desire to hang onto somebody's hand.* They're judging a two-and-half year old toddler in unfamiliar circumstances. I understand why she hated them. I hate them, too.

Enclosed with the documents is David's school paper, scrawled by hand in red ink and entitled, *Possible Goals of an Ecosystem Model: The differences in concepts of realism and generality matrices and phase diagrams.* Periodically, Mother would thrust this academic paper at me. It was Mother's proof of David's genius. To me it looked copied. I didn't believe David wrote it. I saw it as evidence of the unbearable pressure put upon him to perform at school.

\*

One of David's poems was printed in the 1997 edition of *Through the Looking Glass,* a large hardcover book from The National Library of Poetry. David has written his name and a page number inside the cover.

*DAVID BRENNER*
*page 319*

Page 319 is the page where David's poem appears. In the back of the book are sixty-five pages of biographical notes. David Brenner is not among them. David Brenner has no notes. The notes suggest that none of the poets has ever published. I believe Mother paid for the inclusion of David's poem. I believe all the poets paid. Great poets too have had to pay for publication. William Carlos Williams paid for his first books of poems.

The biographical notes list the poets' date of birth and profession, their membership in clubs and organizations. For example, VOLUNTEER BEYOND EXCELLENCE BY HOPEMONT HOSPITAL; or RETIRED PHILADELPHIA POLICE OFFICER; or NATIONAL ARTISTIC ROLLER SKATING CHAMPION. There are both professional and personal notes. Many notes are religious and speak of God.

I'm interested in these poets. I'm glad there's a place where they can get validation for writing poems.

*UNTITLED*

*The beauty of women
is the nature of life
I see the lightness of the
Blueness of her eyes as
I face the day goes
on, the light of the dawn
goes on with blueness of
her eyes.*

*I saw the scenes
of a jail that I was
sentenced to without
a godless trial
I blast the days
through dramatic
experience
wish I was born
with living or dead*

David Brenner

# 35

# THE FALL

After I return to California, I receive a call from the sister of my friend Moe Slotin. Moe lives in Savannah. He lives with his wife and daughter. When the voice says, "This is Moe's sister," my heart falls into my stomach. I think something must be wrong. Then I chastise myself. I remember that my mother has recently died. I am burdened with the affairs of death. Instead, I rearrange my thoughts. I think Moe has given his sister my number for a practical reason. I have never met Moe's sister, but I think she must be coming to San Francisco. Or she needs advice on writing and publishing. I am wrong. *Heart falling into my stomach* is exactly right. She has called to tell me that Moe is dead. She says he was probably sick for months or more. When he finally went to the doctor, the cancer was everywhere. They couldn't tell where it started. Moe's sister is calm when she says these things. She is occupying herself. Her call to me is a way to occupy herself. "He died peacefully," she says.

I tell her that I expected to see Moe in Atlanta at my mother's funeral. I remark how trustworthy and dependable Moe was. That's why I thought I'd see him in Atlanta.

"Moe went to the doctor the week you were in

Atlanta," she says. "He wasn't feeling well. That's when they found the cancer."

Whenever I'd call Moe, day or night, weekend or weekday, in New York or Savannah, he'd answer, "Hey!" It was an endearing habit. He'd pick up the phone and say, "Hey!" Like he knew it was you and was waiting for you to call. Moe treated everyone like a friend.

I thank Moe's sister and hang up. I regard the telephone with disbelief. I look at the phone as if it's alive. Like the voice who told me Moe is dead is still inside the phone. Mother's death, Moe's death, the terror of September 11th, Joanna's distance in New York, Felix's brother's mental breakdown, my friend Dede's cancer, it's too much. But I've already learned something about life. Life doesn't care if it's too much.

In late October, a social worker calls. She's calling from Bright Beginnings. She's calling me because I'm David's next of kin. The social worker says, "David fell down. He tripped over a chain across the driveway. He fell and broke his ankle. We called an ambulance as soon as David fell."

David is in the hospital with a broken ankle. After we hang up, I call the hospital. I speak to the doctor on duty. I explain that David is schizophrenic. I explain about his meds. I'm concerned about David's meds. I'm concerned that Bright Beginnings has been negligent. In fact, Bright Beginnings hasn't notified the hospital about David's medication for schizophrenia.

David's break is complicated. The doctors can't put on a cast until they operate. They can't operate until the swelling goes down. I prepare to return to Atlanta. I call my cousin Nancy. She'll drive down from Franklin to Atlanta and meet me.

I get on the late morning Delta flight to Atlanta. Since May it's the fifth time I've flown to Atlanta. Now it's November. The leaves are mostly gone. The air has a hollow feeling. Not the heavy, sweet, portentous, wet, yielding, cruel, noisy air of summer. It's hollow and thin air, hollowed out by the November cold. The sky, the air, the buildings, everything is gray and mute and cold.

I don't stay with Nancy's daughter in her condo. I stay at a hotel in Buckhead. I like hotels. I like having an empty place to sleep and think. I can swim in the pool. I can soak in the Jacuzzi. Nancy is nearby, but I don't have to depend on Nancy. I can hop on MARTA and go to the hospital by myself.

David is at Grady Hospital, the city's public hospital in downtown Atlanta. Grady is the fifth largest public hospital in the country, filled with many indigent patients. David is an indigent patient. He's on SSI, a federal welfare program for the disabled. David's leg is elevated by pulleys. He's not allowed to leave the bed. He fell out of bed and broke his wrist. Not only his ankle but his wrist is broken. That's why he can't leave the bed. He fell trying to get out of bed. The bed is blocked with restraining bars. He has been put into diapers. He's uncomfortable but glad to see me. He's glad I'm here.

I talk to the orthopedic team. They will put a steel plate in David's ankle. They will put a steel plate in David's wrist. David's bones are small and fragile. They break easily. The medication he takes has weakened his bones.

All day David lies in bed, gazing at the window or wall. He doesn't read. He doesn't look at TV. He doesn't like TV. I stay at the hospital and talk to David. We aren't at ease talking, but he knows I'm here to help him.

"Are you sad about Mother?" I ask David.

"Sometimes I miss her," he says. "Sometimes I think about her."

We both know the situation is calmer without her.

"Do you want anything?" I ask.

"Cookies and soda," he says.

I bring him cookies and Cokes.

I talk to David's nurses. Some are sweet and energetic. Others tired, indifferent, or preoccupied. I know a little about nurses from Michael's stroke. After Michael's stroke, he was taken to Georgetown University Hospital in Washington, D. C. For a week, I lived in Michael's hospital room. I slept on a cot. I ate hospital food. I often wore a hospital gown. I met all kinds of nurses.

David calls his nurses *sweetheart*. As they scurry down the hall, he calls from his bed, "Hello, sweetheart!"

I contact Bright Beginnings. They have not communicated well with the hospital. They can't explain the presence of the chain where David tripped. They're defensive about the chain. They aren't friendly. They aren't helpful. Maybe they think I plan to sue.

Some of David's friends from Bright Beginnings have visited him with handmade GET WELL cards. He's pleased to show me the cards. Together, we look at the cards. But after thirteen years of living at Bright Beginnings, no staff member has visited David.

In the past, I suppressed my poor opinion of Bright Beginnings. It was Mother who chose where David lived. The decisions about David were hers. Although the social workers are kind, the director is not. David has told me the director doesn't like him. The director's animosity may have been caused or aggravated by his history with Mother. It's only a guess, but Mother probably hounded the director. In turn, he took it out on David.

I suppressed my opinion because I didn't know where David would go. And he insisted he was happy there. He insisted that he didn't want to move or alter his routine. Now he doesn't want me to complain or meddle. However, my opinion is no longer suppressed. My suspicions are confirmed. Bright Beginnings wants nothing to do with David. Bright Beginnings cares nothing about David. They offer me no guidance, no suggestions, no sympathy.

In Atlanta I take care of other business. I have to see my lawyer. I have to go to probate court. I have to arrange to sell the condo. It's tedious business. David is tedious business. I don't know how I'll manage as David's guardian. When I leave David, I promise to return soon.

## 36

## THE NEXT BLOW

In early December, my son Felix receives a call from Brooklyn. A stranger calls and leaves a message. "Do you know Jesse Rodefer?" That's the message. The caller asks to please call this number if Felix knows Jesse Rodefer.

Of course, Felix knows Jesse. Jesse is Felix's half-brother, one of two older half-brothers and a younger half-brother, all sons of Stephen Rodefer. The stranger in Brooklyn lives with Jesse. He shares a flat with Jesse. The stranger found Felix's name and a San Francisco number on a scrap of paper. The stranger called Felix. He doesn't know Felix. He doesn't know Jesse and Felix are brothers. They have different last names. He calls because Jesse is locked in his room. He's concerned about Jesse. He's trying to help Jesse. The caller says in the message, "There is something wrong with Jesse." He has tried to call Jesse's father in Paris without success. Aside from Stephen's number in Paris, Felix's number is the only number he has found.

Felix notifies his oldest brother Benjamin. "There's something wrong with Jesse," he tells Benjamin. Felix calls me. "There's something wrong with Jesse." We all know something is wrong. We love Jesse and know something is wrong. A year or so ago, Jesse had a breakdown. He had to be taken by ambulance from his uncle's house in Washington, D.C. No one knew what was wrong with Jesse. After he was released from the hospital, Jesse's mother took him home to New Mexico. He was taken to specialists. He was given tests and put on anti-psychotic medication.

Jesse pulled himself together. He worked a little and tried to fathom a future. He didn't want to stay in New Mexico. He didn't want to take medication. He took himself off the drugs and had another episode.

Jesse wanted to go to New York. Jesse was thirty-five years old, a grown man. When he decided to go to New York, no one wanted to tell Jesse that he couldn't go. They believed Jesse was an adult who could make his own decisions. I think they also let him go because they didn't want to admit that Jesse was sick. Jesse had been a gifted boy—a scholar, a musician, an athlete who graduated with honors from Harvard. No one wanted to admit something was wrong.

"I'll drive Jesse to New York," his brother Benjamin said.

Jesse had already lived in New York. He already knew his way around. No one informed Jesse's housemates about his condition. No one said, "Please watch over Jesse." They hoped nothing was really wrong. They hoped that what happened was really over. Jesse's father didn't mention it. Jesse's brother didn't mention it. They decided it was private. Jesse's mental health was private family business. It would violate Jesse to tell other people. It would stigmatize Jesse. Jesse's condition was secret. They kept it secret. They pressed upon me, "It's a secret." They called me to make sure I knew it was a secret.

I muttered under my breath, "It will be a disaster." I muttered to my children, "It will be a disaster." I said nothing to Jesse's mother or father. I hardly know Jesse's mother. I don't have a relationship with Jesse's mother. I rarely speak to Jesse's father. The decision was their business. No one asked my opinion. I didn't offer my opinion. I knew my opinion would not be welcome. Although I wasn't included in their family business, I should have spoken out. What I had that they didn't was an intimate knowledge of mental illness. I had David.

In July I went to New York. Instead of going to see Mother in Atlanta, I went to New York to see my daughter Joanna. I missed my daughter. I told her, "While I'm here, I only want to walk across the Brooklyn Bridge and see Jesse."

Joanna and I spent an afternoon with Jesse. I was happy to spend a few hours with him. We were all happy to be together. At lunch he ate like a famished man. Then we walked to a park in the West Village. Jesse was a little nervous, a little restless, but he was happy to see us. He laughed a lot. He'd say something slightly off and laugh a loud, boyish laugh. He made me laugh. I laughed when he laughed. I thought it meant Jesse was okay. A little lost but okay.

After Felix got the call, Benjamin took over. Benjamin called his mother. Jesse's mother called New York. Jesse's mother reassured Jesse that someone was coming to help him.

Benjamin flew immediately to New York. When he arrived in Brooklyn, Jesse was gone. Jesse was out. He'd gone to a jazz club in Manhattan. In the morning, he hadn't come home. Benjamin began to look for Jesse. He went to the jazz club where Jesse liked to hang out.

Jesse's friends told Benjamin, "He was here last night." They said, "He wasn't well. He was hot. He was sweating. He was distressed." They said Jesse got so hot that he started to take off his clothes. They said they wanted to call 911.

Jesse told his friends, "I'm going outside to cool off."

The police found Jesse's clothes by the river. They found his shoes and his clothes neatly folded by the river. They didn't find Jesse. No one found Jesse. Everyone thinks Jesse was so hot that he jumped into the river. Everyone thinks Jesse went into the river—not to kill himself but to cool off. Although it was December, he went into the Hudson to cool off. It's easy to drown in the Hudson. The tidal currents in the Hudson are enormous. Jesse went into the river and drowned.

I think about David and Jesse. I can't help but compare them. David was cut off from the world for thirty years.

Mother put David away to protect him from himself and others. She put him away because she couldn't take care of him. It's difficult to care for a mentally ill person. I understand why she couldn't do it. Nonetheless, she controlled everything in David's life. He had no control over anything. He was allowed no decisions of his own. He took whatever was dished out.

With Jesse it was different. His family let him go back into the world. They let him make his own decisions. They believed the psychiatric drugs would protect him. They let him live his own life.

In both cases, it ended badly. Jesse drowned. And David lives a lonely, isolated existence.

## 37

## GOOD AFTER BAD

I'm on the late morning Delta flight from San Francisco to Atlanta. David is still in the hospital. He has been there almost two months. After the operations on his ankle and wrist, he stayed in the hospital. Bright Beginnings wouldn't let him return until he was well. They couldn't take care of him while he convalesced. The hospital tried to find a place to care for David, but there was nothing available. The nursing homes were full. No one would take David, so he was left in the hospital.

Now they've noticed an anomaly. A few days ago, David was rushed to x-ray because his heart rate was elevated. They expected to find an embolism. The x-ray didn't show an embolism but a mass. The mass is lung cancer.

The oncology team says that David must be treated immediately. If not, he will die in a few weeks. His cancer is fast and virulent. It has already spread.

If the nurse at the hospital hadn't paid attention to his heart rate, the cancer could have gone undetected. If David had been in a nursing home or at Bright Beginnings, it's possible that no one would have found the cancer. David would have gotten sick and quickly died. If he hadn't tripped and fell, if he hadn't broken his ankle, if he hadn't been in the hospital, and if this sequence of events hadn't occurred—events I'd later call miracles—he probably would have quickly died. A doctor or a social worker in Atlanta would have called me. Someone would have called to tell me, "Your brother passed away." An anonymous person would have called to say, "Your brother unexpectedly died." In response to my disbelief, they would have explained, "He died of lung cancer." Maybe they would have added, "I'm sorry your brother died."

I would have been surprised. I would have wondered why no one knew about his cancer. I would have blamed Bright Beginnings for not taking care of David. But blame wouldn't have brought David back to life. I would have had to accept that David was dead.

I'd have told friends, "My mentally ill brother in Atlanta died."

I'd have told my children, "Your mentally ill uncle died."

It would have been sad, but it was already sad. I would have put its sadness alongside the other sadnesses. The recent sadnesses of Mother, Jesse, and Moe. The recent sadness of learning that my close friend Dede also has lung cancer. I would have mourned David's passing. But my life, so far away and disconnected from him, would have continued with little interruption. David's death would not have brought me to my knees.

Now I'm in Atlanta to discuss a course of action with

David and the oncology team. Michael has come with me. Michael is a great comfort. He has come to help me make these difficult decisions. Nancy has driven to Atlanta from Franklin. She is a great comfort, too.

When we come into the hospital room, David hops out of bed. He wants to show us he can walk. He wants to show off what he learned in physical therapy. When he hops out of bed, his hospital gown flies open. We laugh because his hospital gown is open, and we can see his naked body. We laugh while David shows us how he can walk down the hall.

Nancy and I lie down with David in his bed. We tease and comfort him. We cuddle beside him. David is happy we've come.

In the afternoon, we go out. We go to buy David food. He has requested cookies, burgers, and Cokes. We go out for lunch and fresh air. It's a raw, cold day. A holiday for Dr. King's birthday. Nearby, we find a diner with home-style Southern food—creamed corn, mashed potatoes, hash browns, stewed okra, green beans, butter beans, lima beans, pork chops, fried chicken, chicken fried steak, and cornbread.

A march for Dr. King passes by the diner. We hurry up and finish so we can join the march. We march with the others to the MLK Memorial on Auburn Avenue. A few hundred of us march. On this cold and gloomy day, the memorial looks gloomy and neglected.

Maybe the gloom is inside me. In April 1968, I was

in Atlanta. I was living with Paige. The night before Dr. King's funeral, I drove back and forth to the airport. In Paige's VW van, I picked up strangers at the airport. Men and women arrived at all hours for Dr. King's funeral. I picked them up at the airport and dropped them off at SCLC headquarters. I was part of a large caravan of taxis and private cars, going back and forth, picking up and dropping off.

Dr. King was killed in April. The funeral was in April. Atlanta's beauty was in full bloom. Azaleas and rhododendrons were in bloom. The bright spring contrasted with the darkness of the occasion. The perfume from the flowers made me sick. I couldn't go to the funeral because I was sick. I was sick and upset from fatigue and heartbreak. Paige urged me to go with him to the funeral. Paige didn't want me to miss such an important historic occasion. But I decided not to go. I didn't want to be in a crowd of people—mourners, journalists, photographers, celebrities. The crowd would turn the funeral into a spectacle. I didn't want to share my grief with anyone. I wanted to guard it. I wanted to keep it inside me. Because of Daddy, I knew how to keep it inside me. I wanted to be alone.

Daddy used to say that I was born the year FDR died. He made it seem that FDR's death was more important than my birth. When I got older, I understood. My birth only affected a few lives, but FDR touched millions. It was the same with Dr. King. His life and death affected the whole world.

The oncology team explains that David's lung cancer has spread to his liver and brain. I talk to David about his choices. Now that he has cancer, his choices are different. His recovery is more complicated than a broken ankle and a broken wrist. I don't want him to stay in Atlanta. I don't want him to return to Bright Beginnings. I want him to come to California.

David understands his situation. He knows what happens to people like him. "If I stay here, they'll throw me away in a nursing home," he says.

"Come to California so I can take care of you," I say.

"Okay, I'll come to California," David says.

I make a plan with the oncology team in Atlanta. They will do one round of chemotherapy. After they treat David, I'll return and pick him up. Michael and I will come to Atlanta and pick him up. I have spoken to Michael. Michael has agreed. We'll come to Atlanta to pick up David and bring him back to live with us. Although Michael hardly knows my brother, he has agreed. It's not easy for Michael, but Michael does the right thing. He does the loving and courageous thing. He makes it easy for me to decide. He lets me open our home to David.

"When he's better," I tell Michael, "I'll find another place for him to live."

That's the plan. First, David will live with us. When the cancer is under control, I'll find a good care home nearby where David can live.

I ask my friend Jane, "Do you think I'm crazy to bring my crazy brother here to live with us?"

"Yes," Jane laughs. Jane's laugh reassures me.

Life is profoundly comical, tragic, and absurd. Now life has risen up and asked—HELP YOUR BROTHER! Now I have a chance to help my brother. Now that our mother is dead, there is a clear and unencumbered way.

I notify my lawyer to expedite the transfer of David's guardianship. I call Bright Beginnings and ask them to pack and ship David's things to our house in Berkeley. I investigate the process of transferring David's SSI benefits from Georgia to California. I locate a nearby cancer treatment center that takes government insurance. I buy a microwave oven so David can prepare his own food. I clean out a closet. I empty a chest of drawers. I prepare for David to come and live with us.

# 38

# FLIGHT

In early February, Michael and I return to Atlanta. Early February is crisp, sunny, and cold. It's a beautiful winter day. When we roll David out of the hospital, it's the beginning of a new life for him. And us. The three of us are starting a new life. We roll David in a wheelchair. We get him into a taxi. We ride to a hotel near the airport. We eat dinner at the hotel. We go to bed early. We sleep in two large beds. David is in one bed, Michael and I in the other. Michael and I sleep close to David.

David is nervous, nervous and shy. He's nervous because his life is about to change. He doesn't know what to expect. He doesn't know what's going to happen. He hasn't flown in 32 years. He doesn't know Michael. He hardly knows me. But now he is in our hands. He has put his life in our hands, and we're taking him to California.

At the airport, David is transferred from a taxi to a wheelchair. The wheelchair allows us to go to the front of the security line. The lines are extremely long. The wait is extremely long. We go immediately to the front of the line.

People stare at David. He attracts attention. People stare at him in the wheelchair and at us because we're with David. I remember how they would stare at David when we were with Mother. In a restaurant or the grocery store, people stared. When they stared, Mother would glare back at them. If they were staring, Mother's glaring made it worse.

But Michael and I aren't anxious. Or defensive. We don't care if people stare. We're glad to be with David. When people see that, they relax and smile. I suppose there are many reasons they smile. Some are probably irritating and inane. Some are probably self-righteous. It probably makes them feel like a good person to smile. We don't care. We only care that we're with David.

David carries a one-way ticket. When we reach the gate, his ticket presents a problem. Since 9/11 one-way tickets are associated with terrorists. David is searched before we can board. His backpack is searched. His body is scanned. He is singled out from other passengers, which terrifies him. He's scared that he won't be able to board the plane. Or go to California. Their search was probably triggered by his one-way ticket. But it's sad they pick on him. He looks completely helpless, completely vulnerable—and they pick on him. Finally, they let him on.

It's a few hours to fly from Atlanta to Oakland. It's an uneventful trip. The drive from Oakland to Berkeley is uneventful, too. When David arrives at the house, he's pleased. He's delighted. He's going to sleep in a private home for the first time in thirty years.

This is the first house I've owned. The first house of my own that I've lived in as an adult. This too is part of the series of miraculous intersections. Mother doubted that I'd ever be able to care for David in my own home. When she visited, I lived in small apartments or cottages. I had two children to support. I shared houses with other families.

Now Michael and I own a home with an empty bedroom that we can share with David. I show David his room. It's a pleasant, sunny room with a double bed and tall double-hung windows that face south. This will be David's room while he's sick. He will live in this room until he gets better. If he survives, then I will find somewhere else for him to live.

When David first comes, I take time off from work. I take a week off. There's a long list of things to do. We must meet with social workers, pick up prescriptions, and shop for toiletries and food.

At the grocery store, I tell David, "Choose whatever you like to eat."

He chooses canned and frozen foods, Hot Pockets, and frozen turkey dinners. He's accustomed to processed food served in institutions. We tend to eat late. David likes to eat early. We eat mostly vegetarian fare. David likes meat. He doesn't have to eat what or when we eat. I tell him to do whatever he wants. I want him to feel comfortable. I want him to feel this is his home.

David demands very little. He doesn't watch TV. He

doesn't like movies. He doesn't read books or look at magazines. He doesn't play cards or games. His favorite pastime is to listen to old rock & roll. David calls it "Georgia trash." By the bed is a radio. David listens to the station that plays Oldies But Goldies. He loves the R&B singers best—Ray Charles, Little Richard, Fats Domino, Otis Redding, James Brown.

I got my first radio in sixth grade. The radio was by my bed. I listened to it day and night. I don't remember if David had a radio. I ask him if he had a radio as a boy.

"I had nothing," he says.

If he's not in his room, David sits on our mother's settee. A small sofa covered in dark cut-velvet with a bargello pattern. He sits in the corner and looks out the big picture window at the garden.

"What are you thinking?" I ask him.

"Calming thoughts," he says. He has learned to think calming thoughts.

David often sings. The singing is quiet but constant. Whenever I come into the room, he greets me warmly. He asks me sweetly, "How ya doing?" Then he bursts into song. When he sings, he makes gestures that imitate performers. Not rock singers but old crooners. He cocks his head, extends his arm, and lifts his hand like a professional singer.

*Strangers in the night*
*Dodadodado*

*Strangers in the night*
*Dodadodado*
*Something in your eyes*
*Something in your smile*
*Dodadodadododo*

If I ask David how he's doing, he says something positive. He never says, "I feel bad." Many times a day, we exchange niceties, inquiring how the other is doing. He never complains. He says, "Just fine."

David's Southern accent is thick. Some words are garbled. The medication has altered the muscles in his mouth. He has a condition called tardive dyskinesia, which makes it difficult to speak clearly. Tardive dyskinesia is a side effect of his anti-psychotic drug. It makes him stretch his lips and extend his tongue. It makes him move his mouth like another kind of animal.

If the weather is mild, David sits in a wicker chair on the back porch, observing what goes on in the garden. If you're observant, things go on. When I come home, he describes what he has seen. He mostly watches birds, but once a large, unidentified animal crossed the grass. He holds up his bony hands a couple of feet apart to show me.

"This big," he says.

It moved slowly and frightened him. I guess possum. They roam around our yard at night, lumbering over new plants and moving rocks, oblivious and nearly blind. I've never seen one in the day.

We encourage David to walk. We want him to walk and use his ankle. Walking will help strengthen his ankle. While I'm at work, Michael walks with him around the block. Friends come by and walk with him around the block. David isn't comfortable going out of the house. When he walks in the yard, he hurries. He takes mincing steps across the yard. He wants to show how fast he can walk. He wants to get it over with. He doesn't want to relax and stroll around. He wants to hurry and then sit quietly on the porch.

At first, David is anxious. He's worried he might make a mistake. He doesn't know me. He doesn't know what kind of temperament I have. He worries I might be like Mother and yell at him. Nice at first, then flip. I'm sure he worries. It takes a few weeks for him to relax. After a few weeks, he says to me, "You're such a nice person." David likes to say what a nice person I am. After time passes, he realizes I don't yell or curse.

From time to time, I try to get David to discuss our childhood. I'm curious what he thinks about our childhood. I'm interested in what he remembers.

"Things would have been better if Daddy had lived," David says. "If Daddy hadn't had a heart attack, our lives would have been better."

He almost never mentions Mother. He doesn't have a kind word to say about Mother. He's relieved she's out of his life.

At first, David sings all the time. When he's on the settee gazing out the window, he sings. In the morning when he gets up, he lopes into the living room, sits down, and starts to sing. Sometimes it's annoying. Sometimes it drifts upstairs. Sometimes it penetrates the walls. Michael can't restrain himself. He doesn't want to criticize David, but the singing drives him nuts. I want to keep Michael happy and David comfortable. Michael has been generous in the extreme. He has hardly complained. But now he's unnerved. His peace of mind disrupted. David gets on his nerves. He can't listen to the singing or the radio a minute longer.

"Make David stop singing," Michael says.

One evening after work, I sit down beside David. As soon as I sit down, he starts to sing. He starts to chirp and croon. He sings his version of "Strangers in the Night." He doesn't know all the words so he fills in with *dodadodado*. I don't want to hurt David's feelings. I don't want him to feel unwanted, but I make myself think about Michael.

When I sit down, David says, "Step into my office." Then he starts to sing.

"You don't have to sing," I say. "We can have a conversation. Instead of singing, we can talk."

I try to take his hand. He doesn't like to be touched.

"The singing sometimes annoys us," I say gently. "We can sometimes hear it upstairs. Even the birds sometimes stop singing."

"Okay, what do you want to talk about?" he asks.

I'm interested in what David thinks. I'm interested in his viewpoint. I decide to ask a big question.

"What if we talk about the meaning of life?" I ask.
David nods approvingly.
"What do you think is the meaning of life?"
"Singing," he says.

## 39

## VISITS AND VISITATIONS

Giant bugs are common in the South but very unusual in northern California. Ocean winds, summer fog, mild temperatures keep insects away. We're in bed when a giant bug appears. It's fat like a June bug. It flies in crazy circles. It makes crazy noises. Michael and I put down our books to watch. We can't read with the racket. It flies so fast that we can hardly track it. It dives from corner to corner. Then it suddenly disappears. The room is quiet. No bug. No racket.

"That was Mother," I laugh. I laugh, but it's not a joke. Despite being a practical, level-headed person, I think it was Mother.

In the morning, I search for it. I search the floor, the closets, my office shelves. It's gone. Later I tell David about the bug. He doesn't respond. He doesn't want to discuss Mother. He doesn't want to think she has made a visitation. He doesn't want to believe she can come back from the dead. We're superstitious people. We remember when Mother made us chew thread, throw salt, knock on wood. Growing up, we knocked on wood a thousand times. We remember beach vacations, and when it rained, Mother blamed her sister Evelyn. If Mother traveled abroad and the weather was bad, she blamed Evelyn. She said Evelyn tried to ruin everything.

Mother always said we were unlucky people. She was born beautiful and rich. She never had to work. She married the smartest man she ever met. She traveled the world. She became a wonderful painter. But she thought she was unlucky.

"Just my luck," she'd say bitterly. "Just my luck."

True, she suffered. As a child with a severe illness, she suffered. From a sour marriage, David's problems, Daddy's suicide, my virtual abandonment, her estrangement from her sisters, she suffered. Whatever hadn't worked out, she blamed on bad luck.

Soon after David arrives, we begin to visit doctors. I want David to have an internist. Dr. Herb is a lovely woman. She's someone I met long ago. She's married to someone I knew long ago. Dr. Herb takes MediCal patients. She's glad to care for David. She makes him comfortable. She is warm and respectful. David is happy to have Dr. Herb as his doctor.

The oncologist is a different sort. He's careless and brusque. He asks David, like it's a rhetorical question, "Aren't you a little schizophrenic?" He laughs when he asks.

I'm shocked at how he speaks to us. He hurries through the visit, too rushed to make David comfortable. "Deal with my nurse," he tells me.

His nurse will schedule David's chemotherapy. Every few weeks, David will go into the hospital for chemotherapy. In between the rounds of chemotherapy, he'll come home. In between, he'll have radiation on his brain.

My friend Dede is also undergoing chemotherapy for lung cancer. Her cancer has also spread. Instead of radiation, the doctors are using a gamma knife that pinpoints the tiny tumors in her brain.

Dede is one of my oldest and dearest friends. She lives in Laguna Beach. She takes care of her twin boys. She walks. She runs. She swims. She's starting graduate school. She has cancer, but it doesn't interrupt her life.

Dede and I talk every day. She assures me every day that she's doing well. She believes in mind over matter. She believes in the spiritual principles of Eckankar. She thinks she can will the cancer out of her body.

"I'm not going to die," Dede says.

Since I can't leave David, Dede comes to visit us. She comes to meet David and see me. She's strong. She handles the chemotherapy. She handles the gamma knife. She takes hundreds of pills prescribed by naturopaths. She's amazing.

David responds well to chemotherapy, too. He doesn't get sick. He doesn't complain. He likes his hospital room. He likes the hospital food. It's a first-class hospital, not like the public hospital in Atlanta. It's luxurious and light-filled. His favorite nurse is Nancy. David loves his nurse Nancy. He loves his favorite cousin Nancy. At home he sometimes calls me "Nancy."

After the first round of chemotherapy, David returns

home. We revisit the oncologist. Although he's rushed, he now welcomes David. He warms to David. He wants to know how he feels. He wants to cure him. It doesn't take much to change the temperature between people—only a drop or two of kindness.

I apply to a county program that provides help in the home. Although David can shower and feed himself, he needs help. Although Michael checks on David, I worry that he's lonely.

"I'm not lonely," David says. "I never get lonely."

He doesn't mind sitting all day by the window, thinking calming thoughts. He has no complaints. Every day he thanks us for letting him live in our house.

The county qualifies David for in-house aid. The county agrees to pay someone to stay with David a few hours a day. While I'm at work, I want David to have company and eat a good lunch.

"Do you want to take care of David?" I ask Robi.

I was once married to Robi's brother John. I've known Robi for years. Robi is a great guy. He's a musician and mostly works at night. Robi agrees to come on weekdays and take care of David.

Robi is a thoughtful, philosophical man, a cosmological thinker. David becomes part of his cosmology. For Robi, David is an angel. A misunderstood, mistreated angel. Robi believes David possesses a purity missing in the rest of us. Robi is right. I agree with Robi that David is angelic. David is profoundly sweet, profoundly accepting. Neither bitter nor begrudging, he accepts almost anything.

"David is amazing," Robi says.

Robi identifies with David. Robi had a harsh childhood and identifies with David. Robi is accepting like David. Robi believes that Life is trying to teach him, and he is trying to learn. Robi regards David as one of his teachers.

Robi is keen to improve David's diet. He wants David to eat fresh food and drink fresh juice instead of soda. He makes special concoctions and brings over special pills.

David soon starts to complain to me about Robi. David doesn't want to change his diet. He wants to eat Hot Pockets and turkey sandwiches. He wants to drink Cokes. Robi is the only thing he complains about. Robi asks too many questions. Robi wants him to eat healthy food. Robi annoys him.

"I'm his only customer," David says. "I need a vacation from Robi."

David makes fun of Robi. If Robi catches him making fun, Robi laughs, too. Robi has a great sense of humor. Robi knows we're all in the middle of a tragic comedy.

Many friends come to visit David. They visit him with love and warmth. They bring little gifts. Jane brings cookies. Amelie brings healing amulets. Iain and Gillian visit often.

"How do I look?" David asks them. He's obsessed with how he looks.

He's gaunt and thin, but we all say, "You look fine, David. You look just fine."

When visitors stop by, David is in his usual place by the window that overlooks the garden. He salutes his new friends when they arrive. When they come in, he salutes. When they leave, he salutes.

At the grocery store, we try to stand in Dolores' line. Dolores has taken a great liking to David. She thinks he's blessed. She calls him, "Cool little guy." David wears his sunglasses and baseball hat to the grocery store. He brings his cane. He looks every bit like a cool little guy.

Before chemotherapy affects his hair, David regularly needs a proper shave. First, I take him to a beauty salon. That's a mistake. The girl shaves him with a hair clipper. Then I find a real barbershop that uses razors. The barbershop is in a Black neighborhood on Sacramento Street. Lots of people hang out at the barbershop. Inside the shop and on the sidewalk, they hang out. The barbers know everyone. The barbers welcome David. They help him into the high seat. They put pillows behind his neck. They warm his skin with hot towels. They give him a proper shave.

After a few rounds of chemotherapy, David is worn out. He gets out of bed. He gets dressed. But he's worn out. He can't walk around the block. He can only sit in the living room and look out the window. Sometimes he puts a blanket over his head. He uses the blanket to disappear. If friends come by and he wants to hide, he covers his head with a blanket. If he's tired, he ducks into the blanket.

The doctor won't say how long David will live. The doctor simply doesn't know. After chemotherapy and radiation, the cancer may come back. The doctor can't tell us.

Michael and I joke that David will make a full recovery. "We'll die before David," Michael says. "David was supposed to come for a few months, but he stayed for years."

We joke, but it's not funny. We don't want David to die. And we don't want to care for him indefinitely. It's delicate the way we feel about David. I promise again that after David is well enough, I'll find another place for him to live.

Our lives revolve around David. Although we go out, we can't leave town. Michael leaves town for work, but we can't go on vacation. When we go out, we ask David to come. He never wants to come. He doesn't like to go out. The last movie he saw was *Rosemary's Baby*. He never wants to see another movie. He wants to stay home and go to bed early. He gets tired early. His medicine makes him sleepy. The chemotherapy makes him tired.

I worry David will trip when he gets into the shower. He has to step over the rim of the tub. Understandably, he doesn't want me to help him bathe. After he trips once, I ask Robi to help him in the shower. Robi helps and waits for him outside. Once I surprised David. He was still undressed, and I surprised him. We were both embarrassed.

Later he asked me, "What do you think of my peter?"

He laughed, and I laughed, too. "Your peter is beautiful," I told him.

Another time David told me he was scared to look at himself in the mirror. "I'm ugly," he said. He never looks at himself. Maybe that's why he asks others how he looks.

David's birthday is October 24, but I plan a party in May. I want to give a party before he's too weak. As children, we didn't have birthday parties. I want to give him a party that makes up for our childhood. David is pleased with the decorated cake, the bouquet of balloons, the group of friends who bring flowers and gifts. But after a short time, he wishes it were over. He's worn out. It's tiring to be the center of attention. He's glad when everyone leaves.

David now lets me come into his room. At bedtime he invites me to talk to him. He doesn't want me to help him. He doesn't want me to treat him like an invalid. But now he asks for my attention. After he's in bed, I go into his room and sit beside him. I often compliment him. I compliment his singing. I compliment his looks.

"Thank you, thank you," David mumbles. Then he starts to sing.

I say these things to David because he's precious to me. I want him to know he's precious. I say them to make him feel good. But my compliments irritate Michael. Michael thinks my compliments are hypocritical. He doesn't like my boosting David.

"David doesn't look good. David doesn't sing well," Michael says.

To me that's unimportant. To me it has nothing to do with standards of singing. Or conventions of beauty. It's a way to make David feel better. The world has mistreated him and in these small, insignificant ways, I try to make David feel better.

Michael and I disagree. "You're indulgent," Michael says.

David is dying in front of us, and Michael calls me indulgent.

I understand Michael's feelings. I understand he wants my attention. He grew up feeling rejected. His mother never cared for him. His mother was cold and uncaring. Michael has behaved like a prince, but he doesn't like my spoiling David.

When Michael leaves town for work, it's easier. When Michael is away, it's easier. David would never suggest it's easier. David is indebted to Michael. David is grateful to Michael. But when Michael leaves, David and I share the sensation that our childhood lives have been reprieved. We're alone in our pine straw house, a house we've made by scooping pine straw into lines. We're playing under beams of sunlight that fall through the thick pines in our yard on Habersham Road.

"What's wrong with Michael?" David sometimes asks me. After Michael leaves, David asks, "What's wrong with Michael?"

"Michael isn't as unhappy as he looks," I say.

But David is right. Michael is not a cheerful man. He has a great sense of humor, but he's not cheerful. I assure David it has nothing to do with him. If Michael is depressed, it has nothing to do with him.

Despite everything, David is very cheerful. With his difficult life and his cancer, he has reason to be depressed. But he always smiles and sings. He always inquires, "How are you?" If someone coughs or cuts their finger, he asks if they're okay.

I can see how remarkable David is. He's a remarkable person. All the years that Mother pressed him on me, insisting that I admire him, I ignored her. I dismissed her illusions about David. She wanted us to be close. She wanted us to be peers. Her pressure kept me from having a relationship with David. I saw only the damage—his and hers.

In Mother's last years, she asked many times, "What's going to happen to David when I die? What do you intend to do about David?"

She didn't want him to be alone. She didn't want him to feel abandoned. "Will you help David?" she asked me.

"Of course," I told her over and over. "Don't worry. He can always come and live with me."

"Don't be ridiculous!" That's what Mother said at the

suggestion that David could live with me. I was a pauper with two children to raise. My finances were precarious. We often moved. Our homes were small with no room for another person. It seemed unlikely that I could ever keep a promise to let David live with me.

But that's exactly what happened. Mother died, and David lives with me. Now that he's here, I see what Mother wanted me to see. All those years what I couldn't see, I can see now. I see his moments of insight, his consideration of others, his sly humor. I have become his cheerleader and champion.

Most remarkable is David's receptivity. I see why receptivity is a form of enlightenment. David accepts. Without resentment, he accepts. He's receptive because life has always been beyond his control. A raft in the force of a strong current without a way to steer. Without a way to stop. That has been David's life. As a result, he doesn't struggle. Maybe he struggled once. Maybe he struggled against the tyrants who took care of him. And against Mother. But he doesn't struggle with me. If something bothers him, if Michael or Robi bothers him, he simply shrugs and goes on.

"Your Uncle David is amazing," I tell my children. I press David on Michael. I repeat his remarks to friends. I applaud his wit. I've taken up my mother's crusade.

# 40

# TIME OFF

I want to be with David. I want to care for David. I don't want to be away all day at work. I want to be home to take care of David. I give notice in June, initiating the search for my replacement.

David's oncologist has wonderful news for us. He comes into the examination room and says, "I have wonderful news. The chemotherapy worked. The cancer is gone from David's liver and nearly gone from David's lungs."

David is weak from the treatments, but he's very happy. He cries out when he hears the news. He cries out and leaps up in his feeble way to pump the doctor's hand.

Our daily rhythms continue. The summer fog rolls in and out. The roses bloom, wither, and bloom. Mail gets delivered. On Saturdays we walk to the Farmers' Market with David. Our cousin Nancy travels from North Carolina to visit. My daughter Joanna travels from New York to visit. My friend Gloria returns from teaching in New Mexico. While she was away, her younger brother David had a heart attack and died. He was a young man and died. She's also having problems with her boyfriend. She's mourning her brother and upset about her boyfriend.

I talk to Gloria about her troubles. Sometimes it's hard to talk to her and take care of David. I'm still going to work and sometimes too tired to talk. David competes with her for my attention. He's possessive of my attention.

"My friend is having a rough time," I say.

I explain to David about her dead brother, her distant boyfriend, her crazy mother. He's unsympathetic. What's *rough* compared to his life?

David starts calling her "the mental case." Whenever the phone rings, he says, "It's the mental case." If I'm on the phone, he asks, "Are you talking to the mental case?"

It's one of David's sly jokes, but once he meets Gloria—and sees how pretty and vivacious she is—his resentment evaporates. He adores her. He lavishes her with compliments. He calls her "Miss America." He acts like they're engaged. They sit on the back porch and hold hands. He makes romantic gestures and mutters romantic endearments. He cheers and amuses her. They cheer and amuse each other.

Friends and family stop by. They care for David in their own way. When they come, I sit and visit. I make tea and serve cookies. I watch them tend to David. I watch them work out something about their own lives because David is in theirs.

In early September, we return to the doctor. The news is not so good.

"The cancer is back," the doctor says.

Most of it went away, but now it's back. David has already made up his mind. If the cancer comes back, he won't have further treatments. That's his decision. The treatments made him feel terrible. More treatments will make him feel worse. He's saddened by the bad news, but he's not surprised. He knows he's weak. He knows he's sick. It's hard for him to get around. It's hard for him to get up. Everything is an effort.

At the doctor's office, David asks me a favor. He asks that I don't tell Robi about the cancer. "Please don't mention anything to Robi," he says. "Robi will make a federal case. Robi will make me eat raw vegetables."

I don't tell Robi. Robi is a believer. No matter the odds, he believes he can will David back to health. Like Dede, Robi believes his willpower can save David. When I tell my kids, I cry. When I talk to Michael, I cry. David is dying, there's no doubt now. There was never any doubt. He came to California to die. We always knew, but it was so wonderful we forgot.

I need to know what to do. I need to know how to help David. I need to know how to help myself.

A social worker comes to observe David. She comes to ascertain if he qualifies for additional help. She is moved by David. She is moved by us.

"You and Michael have done a great thing," she says.

"You and Michael have done a great thing," others say.

Yes, we've provided him with a bed and Hot Pockets

and affection. We've given him a place to live and soon a place to die. But I don't think it's so great. I think what David has done is greater. David has allowed me to reprieve our childhood. He has given me the chance to rectify my decades of life without him. Together, we have rectified these years. He and I are together again. We are together in my home. A lovely home. There are no crazy people here. There is no savage fighting here. I can determine how David is treated. I can dictate the kindness and respect with which he is treated. Together, we have rewritten how it was going to be. We have altered his fate and mine. He has been removed from a lonely place where he was destined to live out his days. And dropped inside another life. He has been dropped inside a community where he's not treated like a freak, or a burden, or a misfit. For perhaps the first time, David has been loved for who he is.

# 41

# LEGACY

David wants to make a will. He wants to leave us money. He's proud to have money to give away. He has never had his own money. He has never had the right to make decisions about money. Every decision about money was made by his caretakers, the government, and Mother. He was considered incompetent. Now he can choose to give away money. He wants to leave money to Nancy, Felix, Joanna, Michael, and me. Because Felix is a lawyer, David asks him to make a will. David dictates, and Felix writes it down.

I have to ask David difficult questions.

"Do you want to be cremated?"

No, he does not want to be cremated.

"Do you want to be buried in Atlanta?"

No, he does not want his body to fly on an airplane. He does not want to be buried in the family plot near Mother.

"I'll do whatever you want," I tell him. "You can be buried here."

David is pleased. We're both pleased.

Oakland's Mountain View Cemetery is a short distance from our house. It's a beautiful cemetery designed by Frederick Law Olmsted. It's an historical landmark filled with the graves and sepulchers of illustrious families. It's also a bird sanctuary and a park.

It's possible to buy a plot at the edge of the oldest and most beautiful section of the cemetery. I pick out a site for David along a graceful winding road. There's a view of San Francisco Bay. Nearby are old trees, fountains, urns, and obelisks. I show the cemetery's brochure to David. We speak frankly about death. We speak like adults. I don't pretend. David doesn't pretend.

"We all have to die someday," he says.

"Would you like to see the cemetery?" I ask. "Or perhaps that's too depressing."

"I'm used to everything," David says.

"Tomorrow we'll go," I say.

We never go. He's too weak to go. It's too much effort to leave the house.

"What will you wear to the funeral?" he asks me.

"Something you'd like," I say.

He asks me to describe my outfit. Then I show him the clothes—the black skirt and black fitted jacket, the jewelry and heels. He's pleased. He approves.

Every evening I ask what he wants for dinner. He always requests hot turkey, mashed potatoes, and gravy. I buy his dinner at Brennan's, an Irish bar and cafeteria in the west section of Berkeley. I drive or walk down University Avenue to Brennan's.

Chinese men work behind the steam plates. After a few days, they recognize me. They know my order—

white meat only, no cranberry sauce, extra dressing. Young Latinas operate the cash register. They recognize me, too. I tell one of the girls about my brother. I tell her the take-out order is for my brother.

"He's dying," I say. When I stop coming, she'll know my brother is dead.

One evening David and I sit together on the settee next to the picture window. He curls his arms around a pillow. He stretches out his skinny legs. He's tiny—bald and tiny. I hunch at the other end. When I look at him, I get weepy. I'm about to lose David again.

He mocks me, "Boohoo! Boohoo!"

He says, "We all don't live forever."

He sings, "Ain't That a Shame."

When I cry, he says, "You better find someone to talk to."

I don't know if he means a therapist. Or that after he dies, I'll be alone. I don't ask what he means. For a minute, it's funny. Then I cry again.

I ask David to forgive me for leaving him. "I had to leave," I say. "I had to leave Atlanta and go away."

David brushes aside my apology. It's what happened. There's nothing to discuss.

"I had a very crappy life," he says. That's how he puts it. "I had a crappy life. I don't want a crappy death. After all the hell I went through, I don't want a crappy death."

The only time that David cries is when he says, "I don't want to leave my family." Tears run down his face.

His little chest heaves and shakes. "I don't want to leave my family."

*My family*, he says emphatically. I hear how proud he is to have a family. He has a real family—a real and loving family. He's not so different. He's like other people. He has a family. A loving family.

# 42

# HELP!

David can't get up. He can't get out of bed. He can't lift himself for the bathroom. He can't bathe. He can't dress.

Michael carries him to the bathroom. When he needs to get up, he rings a bell. Upstairs, I hear the bell. Michael sleeps through everything, but I hear the bell. When David rings the bell, I wake Michael. Michael stumbles downstairs and carries David to the bathroom.

Since David came to live here, I sleep poorly. I always hear him. His room is directly below ours. I hear him through the floor. Every morning he used to make a thump. His feet made a thump when he climbed out of bed. He thumped his way out the bedroom door and slammed it. Now he can't get up. I don't hear David's thumps and slams anymore. It's another sign. I wish they'd return to annoy me.

When I sleep, I'm always listening for David. I'm listening for the bell. I'm tired all the time. Michael can't always be home to lift and carry David. I can't carry him myself. I don't want to call hospice. Calling hospice will confirm that David is dying. But I can't think of anything else to do.

"Can someone come and stay with David?" I ask the county's hospice agency.

"We don't have the resources," they say.

They can send a nurse to assess David's needs. That's all they can do. The family is expected to manage the care. I'm expected to care for David. I'm surprised hospice can't do more. Angry and surprised, I thought hospice meant something more. I thought hospice meant help.

The hospice nurse arrives full of cheer. He's an exuberant man. "I adore your house!" he says. He chats about the house, nursing, travel, food. He is chatty and curious. He wants to know about us and the house. He's not so interested in David.

I see how he irritates David. David is lying on the settee. He's watching the nurse pay attention to me. I direct the nurse away from me to David. I prompt him to think about David. The nurse is here to care about David. Finally, he makes a few suggestions. He writes an order for a hospital bed and a commode. We'll move David's bed out of his room and replace it with a hospital bed. We'll put the commode by the bed. The nurse prescribes oxygen to make David comfortable. "Oxygen helps," he says. He writes a prescription for morphine. If David is in pain, liquid morphine will be on hand. If David can't breathe, morphine will help. A woman from hospice will come to bathe David.

The nurse gives me a list of referrals for an in-house nursing aide. He hands me the list. He can't recommend any. I have to research their qualifications and cost.

He gives me a number for volunteers to sit with David. He can't recommend any volunteers. After an hour, the nurse leaves.

"Good luck," he says cheerfully.

Is that it? I ask myself.

I call the number for volunteers. I'm given a name.

"I'm glad to sit with him," the volunteer says.

The next day, she arrives. I welcome her inside. I introduce her to David. She's also charmed by the house. She wants to talk about the furniture and the garden.

I regard her blankly. I don't want to converse. I have no interest in conversing. It's not a social visit. I only called because I need to run errands.

"I'm a widow," she says. She volunteers for hospice because she's lonely. "I need to get out of the house," she says.

I'm angry that hospice is unhelpful. I'm angry that my brother is dying. I'm angry that I have to put up with a foolish woman and a silly nurse.

I leave the volunteer with David. I leave for a short while. I don't leave for long. She's too old. She can't possibly lift David. She shows no interest in David.

After a quarter of an hour, I return. "Thank you," I tell her.

"When will you call again?" she asks.

"Thank you," I say. I don't intend to call again

Another day passes. Another hospice nurse arrives. Not a cheerful, chatty man but a woman who is impersonal, methodical, and kind. In other words, exactly right.

"This is inadequate," I say. "I need more help."

"We assumed you had help," she says.

I'm dismayed. Why would anyone assume?

"It shouldn't be called hospice," I complain.

"There's a program," she says.

The nurse knows someone she can highly recommend. She'll get back to me. She'll arrange the paperwork. I'll have help.

## 43

## THE LAST DAY

The woman sent by hospice is wonderful. She laughs but isn't foolish. She chats but isn't inane. She's a humane woman who devotes herself to the dying. She has been in the house for several days. She has stayed into the night. She comforts David and me. She comes whenever we need her. She comes so we can sleep. She's a great help and solace.

There is also something mystical about her. She's very young—not older than 20-something. But she's gifted. She's in touch with the other side. She knows things we don't. She sits with the dying. She helps the dying cross from life to death.

It's the morning of October 14th. It's ten days before David's fifty-second birthday. For breakfast he eats a hot dog. A hot dog is the last thing David eats. Hot dogs are his favorite food. Up until the end, he can eat a hot dog.

That evening David is in bed. His chest heaves with heaviness. He breathes with heaviness. He doesn't talk. I sit beside him.

"I love you," I tell him. "You are a blessing in my life." These are the truths I tell David.

After midnight Michael goes upstairs. I follow. Michael is in bed. He isn't sleeping. He's resting. We're both tired and weary. We need to sleep, but this night isn't for sleeping. We lie down to prepare for what's next.

When I lie down by Michael, he gets up and goes downstairs. After a few moments, he shouts, "Summer! Summer! Summer! Summer!"

His voice startles me. It's filled with command, alarm, surprise. I know what his voice means. I tumble down the steps.

"David is dead," Michael says. He holds me. He holds me close. He's crying because he loves David. He has come to love David.

"David has passed," our helper says.

I look at David. I look at them. They tell me that David is dead, but I don't believe them. I'm in a state of disbelief. For hours we've expected David to die, but now I don't believe what they say. He looks so calm. He looks so content. I think he must be getting well. I think the calmness and contentment mean he's getting well.

I sit with him. I hold his bony fingers. It's true, they're lifeless. I hold his hand, his lifeless hand. He's so peaceful. I'm happy for him. I'm happy he's at peace. If only he could have had peace in life. Why didn't he have peace when he was alive? His life was cruel almost to the end. That's what I think. I'm happy he's at peace *and*—I wish he were alive. Despite his suffering, I wish he were with me.

## 44

# FINAL RITES

In the early morning hours, David is taken away. A hearse comes and takes David away. Two men have driven over an hour to take David away. They dress him in a shroud and take him away. David is dead. David is gone.

I see the future. I see the misery of the future. The days ahead will be long and miserable—and filled with decisions. I will have to make decisions. All I want is to move through the decisions so I can rest and mourn David.

Michael and Felix help, but I must make the final decisions. However, I don't have to be available. I don't have to answer the phone. I don't have to talk to anyone. I only have to make decisions.

I select a funeral home. It's "Family-Owned for Three Generations," not part of a chain or corporation. Michael, Felix, and I arrive at the funeral home, where the pudgy director greets us. The drab beige walls, the artificial flowers, the shabby office, the drawn shades are the predictable customs of death. But they're also a parody. I start to laugh. I laugh at the customs of death. If I laugh, no one will blame me. Queer behavior is part of the customs, too.

In the director's office, I'm asked to complete David's Death Certificate. I'm asked for David's occupation. The question puzzles me.

I turn to Michael and Felix. "Occupation?"

We try to figure out how to answer. David was sick all his life, too sick to have an occupation. But he did *occupy* a life. He occupied a measurement of time from October 24, 1949 to October 15, 2002. He occupied space in Atlanta, Italy, and Berkeley.

"Singer!" Felix exclaims.

We applaud the choice. It's a wonderful choice. SINGER now fills the blank for David Brenner's "occupation" on his Death Certificate.

At home I meet with the rabbi. She is lovely and young. She will conduct the service. We will meet her at the entrance to the cemetery. We will walk behind the hearse. She will lead the funeral procession by foot from the entrance of the cemetery through the alley of trees, up and around the winding road to David's grave. I'm in favor of walking. Walking is the right way to honor the dead.

"We aren't well-versed in Jewish customs," I tell the rabbi. She understands. She'll make a service that balances Hebrew and English.

After we finish walking, we'll stop at the open grave. While she conducts the service, we'll be able to look out at the waters of the bay and up at the sky. There's an open, heavenly feeling on the hill where David will be buried.

Joanna is flying home from New York for the service. Nancy is flying in from North Carolina for the service. My cousin Gail is out of the country, but her two daughters Amy and Lisa will come. My friend Lianne will come from LA. Felix will write the eulogy. Joanna will read David's poem. Afterwards people will gather at the house. I have ordered platters of food. Friends and family will come to the house. We will gather to honor David.

I can't bear the thought of it. I don't know how I'll get through it. I don't want to see any of them. Except for my children, Michael, and Nancy, I don't want anyone near me. I dread the day, but I'm in mourning. The custom of mourning permits anything. I can do anything. At home I can excuse myself. I can go upstairs. If it's dreadful, I will go upstairs. Everyone will understand. If I want to be alone, they will understand.

When the day arrives, I put on my fine black clothes. The outfit I promised David that I would wear. We drive to the cemetery. Gathered between the fountain and gate are family and friends. The rabbi is there. The hearse with the casket is waiting, ready to deliver David to his grave.

Nancy, Michael, and I walk together. Felix and Joanna walk with us. We are the family. We cluster together as the family. We're in front. In black and in mourning, we walk behind the rabbi who walks behind the hearse.

At the grave, six men lift the casket from the hearse.

These men are friends and family. The casket is heavy. It's pine without ornamentation. A plain pine box. They slip the box onto an elevated metal platform inside the grave.

Nancy and I face the rabbi. We stand close together, side by side and touching. We stand like two wings of something invisible. We are first cousins, connected as if we belong to the same body. That's how close we feel. That's how close we are. We are one body. She is one wing, and I am the other.

When Felix reads the eulogy, we laugh like one person. Nancy and I laugh because the eulogy is filled with wit—wit, warmth, and love. It makes us laugh. I'm proud of Felix, proud he can make us laugh. Joanna is next to Felix. She is beautiful. She reads David's poem with feeling and understanding. She stands beside us, a young and beautiful creature. There is something untouchable about her. She was born wise.

Julia is Gloria's young daughter. She has written a poem. She reads the poem aloud. She reads the poem to me. Julia was affected by David. She'd never met anyone like David. He was briefly in her world. David affected her emotionally. His isolation and loneliness, his reconnection to his lost family, affected her.

Young Zia lays her bouquet of star chrysanthemums on David's grave. Zia met David, too. She came to visit with her mother Chic. She drew him pictures. But David wasn't interested. Children didn't charm him. Maybe because he was almost a child himself.

The service is over sooner than I expect. I'm relieved. Soon the day will be over. The end of the day is all I can think of. Soon we are home. A few dozen people arrive to spend the afternoon. The caterer misplaced the order so the food is delayed. But that small mishap has passed. There is food to eat, beverages to drink, simple but ample.

In fact, it's bearable. Socializing is bearable. I don't go upstairs. I don't excuse myself. It's enjoyable. I find it enjoyable to be with family and friends, eating, drinking, talking. That's part of the mourning customs. I share these precious, difficult moments with people I love.

During the afternoon, I put on David's favorite music. He called the music "Georgia trash." I crank up the volume. I crank it as high as it can go. The sound blasts from the machine. Everyone stops. They stare in shock. "It's a mistake," their expressions say. The volume and choice of music must be a mistake.

Little Richard's voice nearly cracks the ceiling. I remember when my cousin Larry's record "Sounds of Sebring" cracked my aunt's ceiling. I remember when Lockheed jets used to crack the sound barrier. The music blasts across the room and into the garden. Little Richard's song is wild and crazy. When I hear it, I go wild and crazy, too. I let go. All of me lets go. I begin to dance. I shimmy like David. He didn't move his feet but shimmied his arms and grinned. He always grinned.

I shimmy, imitating him. And then I take off. I dance

as if possessed. I dance as if no one's watching. I dance like a wild woman. I dance crazy and hard. I dance for David. I feel his spirit inhabiting me. I shake my entire body and laugh. I'm nearly hysterical with laughter. The music overtakes me. The spirit comes in—and I shake. Little Richard and little David have jumped inside me.

## 45

## DUST

A month passes. We arrive in New York. We've come for Thanksgiving. We've come to celebrate Thanksgiving at my cousin Gail's house in New Jersey. We've come to visit Joanna in Brooklyn. My father's sister Aunt Bessie and her husband Uncle Julius arrive from South Carolina. Their son Ron and his wife Evans arrive from North Carolina. Michael, Felix, and I fly from California. Joanna's dad John has driven from Connecticut with a surfboard on top of his vintage Mercedes sedan. It's late November, but he carries his surfboard everywhere. John will join us for Thanksgiving. We're here to gather at my cousin's house.

We left David behind. If he had lived, he'd have traveled with us. We talked about it. It was pleasurable to talk about it with David. He remembered New York. As a boy, he had been in New York with Mother. After we lived in Italy, he had been in New York with me.

"I'd like to go to New York," he said.

If David had been well enough, he would have come. I think we both knew he wouldn't make it. After the cancer returned, we knew he wouldn't live long.

The day before Thanksgiving, we go Uptown. We take the subway up the East side to the Guggenheim

Museum. Mother once said about her art, *If they won't take my paintings when I'm alive, they can have me when I'm dead.*

We have a few of her ashes with us. We arrive at the Guggenheim to honor Mother's joke. Humor and art were the best parts of her. It's good she can still make us laugh.

At the museum, we decide not to go in. We don't need to go in. We don't need to sprinkle a few ashes inside. After all, it's a gesture. It's a joke. A few ashes on the outside are good enough.

Felix warns us to be careful. He appreciates the joke, but he warns us. He wants us to be inconspicuous. He wants us to be discrete. Felix is right. People are terrified of anything that resembles white powder. White powder suggests anthrax. Anthrax has recently been sent in envelopes to target various people. It's a dangerous, deadly substance.

We have a good laugh. We imagine being arrested for sprinkling gray-white powder. We imagine the officials examining the powder for anthrax. And their alarm when they learn it's human remains. We howl with laughter. Once we start to laugh, it's hard to be inconspicuous.

If asked, it would be hard to explain why I'm sprinkling my mother's ashes outside the Guggenheim. If forced to explain, the story would be long and convoluted. It would include my industrious immigrant grandfather, my shrewd and elegant grandmother, my beautiful and frustrated mother, my brilliant and tragic father, my precious and damaged brother, and then— then what?

Then I'd say, "Officer, it's only a few grains of ash. A few grains are almost all that's left of my mother's family."

I'd say, "There isn't enough to collect in your hand, not even to fill a thimble."

I'd point to a building, a bus, a window, a tree.

"See," I'd say. "They've already blown from the sidewalk to the street."

Soon they'll be tossed by the wind and dissolved by the rain. Washed and rubbed away, they'll disintegrate until they're nothing but dust.

## ACKNOWLEDGMENTS

That I'm alive in this time and place begins with gratitude to my grandparents and their decision to leave their homeland. Three of them arrived from Eastern Europe on the cusp of the twentieth century. Of their early lives, I know almost nothing. I cling to photographs, a few facts, and fewer legends. Their histories were mostly lost in the world wars or buried in their efforts of assimilation. Precise names and spellings of places and persons are questionable. My grandfathers' names were changed at port of entry—Auerbach (from Tavrig, Russia, now Lithuania) to Abelman; Cavalick (from Novohrad-Volynskyi, Russia, now Ukraine) to Brenner.

Morris Abelman arrived in Atlanta where his older brothers had settled. As he started to prosper, he went to New York to find a bride. He and Anna Aarons married in 1915 and returned to Atlanta. Their children were my mother Rita (b. 1919) and her sisters Evelyn and Betty. Nathan Brenner traveled to Kentucky, and after marrying Rebecca Patterson (née Patlis from Berezbob, an untraceable name presumably in Ukraine), they moved to Hendersonville, N.C. where Rebecca's family owned a mercantile store. My father Eddie (b. 1914) and his sister Bessie were raised there. Rebecca died before I was born, and I only met my father's father a few times.

*Not only do I thank the forebears who marked my fate, I thank my children Felix Angel Brenner (son of Stephen Rodefer), Joanna Bean Martin (daughter of John Bean), their partners Jackie Patterson and Ike Martin, and my grandchildren Julian Martin, Asa Martin, Talia Martin, Georgia Martin, and Beau Brenner, whose fate I've touched. I thank them all for this book.*

For their support and helpful suggestions, I also want to extend my appreciation to Ella Baff, Laura Chester, Gloria Frym, Joseph Matthews, Mitch Sisskind, Michael Weber, Jane White, Geoff Young, and for his meticulous reading Charlie Haas. Thank you to Lynn Adler and Jim Locker for their help with the paintings and photographs.

### The Missing Lover
SUMMER BRENNER

In step with the kaleidoscopic effect of Lewis Warsh's illustrations that muddle sex and identity each time they appear, Summer Brenner captures and releases varying emotional states in every line of *The Missing Lover*. Her prose is endearing, fast-paced, and unwilling to let the concept of love settle into a single qualitative experience.
 — Evan Burkin, *Rain Taxi*

I didn't know I could know her women in love this way or this well—the question of physical life, the candor of spirit. And sometimes her prose flies up in a rush of poetry.
 — Robert Glück

Made in United States
North Haven, CT
29 June 2024

54213749R00168